# Women and the Universa Declaration of Human Ri

Who were the non-Western women delegates who took part in the drafting of the United Nations Charter and the Universal Declaration of Human Rights (UDHR) from 1945 to 1948? Which Member States did these women represent, and in what ways did they push for a more inclusive language than the 'Rights of Man' in the texts? This book provides a gendered historical narrative of human rights from the San Francisco Conference in 1945 to the final vote of the UDHR in the United Nations General Assembly in December 1948. It highlights the contributions by Latin American feminist delegates and the prominent non-Western female representatives from new Member States of the UN.

**Rebecca Adami** is Senior Lecturer at the Department of Education, Stockholm University and Associate Researcher at SOAS University of London.

## Routledge Research in Gender and History

**Women in Magazines**
Research, Representation, Production and Consumption
*Edited by Rachel Ritchie, Sue Hawkins, Nicola Phillips and S. Jay Kleinberg*

**New Perspectives on European Women's Legal History**
*Edited by Sara L. Kimble and Marion Röwekamp*

**Gender and the Representation of Evil**
*Edited by Lynne Fallwell and Keira V. Williams*

**Transgressive Women in Modern Russian and East European Cultures**
From the Bad to the Blasphemous
*Edited by Yana Hashamova, Beth Holmgren and Mark Lipovetsky*

**Catastrophe, Gender and Urban Experience, 1648–1920**
*Edited by Deborah Simonton and Hannu Salmi*

**Women in International and Universal Exhibitions, 1876–1937**
*Edited by Myriam Boussahba-Bravard and Rebecca Rogers*

**Shame and the Anti-Feminist Backlash**
Britain, Ireland and Australia, 1890–1920
*Sharon Crozier-De Rosa*

**Women, Land Rights and Rural Development**
How Much Land Does a Woman Need?
*Esther Kingston-Mann*

**Revisiting Gender in European History, 1400–1800**
*Edited by Elise M. Dermineur, Åsa Karlsson Sjögren and Virginia Langum*

**Women and the Universal Declaration of Human Rights**
*Rebecca Adami*

For a full list of titles in this series, please visit www.routledge.com

# Women and the Universal Declaration of Human Rights

Rebecca Adami

LONDON AND NEW YORK

First published 2019
by Routledge

2 Park Square, Milton Park, Abingdon, Oxfordshire OX14 4RN
52 Vanderbilt Avenue, New York, NY 10017

*Routledge is an imprint of the Taylor & Francis Group, an informa business*

First issued in paperback 2020



*Library of Congress Cataloging-in-Publication Data*
Names: Adami, Rebecca, author.
Title: Women and the Universal Declaration of Human Rights / By Rebecca Adami.
Description: First edition. | New York, NY : Routledge/Taylor & Francis Group, 2019. | Series: Routledge research in gender and history ; 32 | Includes bibliographical references and index.
Identifiers: LCCN 2018031815 (print) | LCCN 2018034203 (ebook) | ISBN 9780429437939 (ebook) | ISBN 9781138345355 (hbk) | ISBN 9780429437939 (ebk)
Subjects: LCSH: Women (International law)—History. | Women—Legal status, laws, etc. | Women's rights. | United Nations. General Assembly. Universal Declaration of Human Rights—History. | United Nations Human Rights Council.
Classification: LCC K644 (ebook) | LCC K644 .A93 2018 (print) | DDC 341.4/8—dc23
LC record available at https://lccn.loc.gov/2018031815

ISBN: 978-1-138-34535-5 (hbk)
ISBN: 978-0-367-62278-7 (pbk)

Typeset in Sabon
by Apex CoVantage, LLC

Printed in the United Kingdom
by Henry Ling Limited

To
any woman or girl
who aspires
to reach higher

According to Maud Eduards[1] women transgress the limit for what is permitted when they act as a group. They increase the definition of what is legitimate experience and what is politics and not.

## Note

1. See further, Maud Eduards, *Rethinking Change: Current Swedish Feminist Research* (Uppsala: Swedish Science Press, 1992).

# Contents

# Figures

# Preface: United

What united the nations was the victory of defeating National Socialism.

The National Socialist Party, known as Nazism in Germany, had denied the basic rights of all deemed a threat to the principle of the primacy of the nation state during the Second World War: Jewish people, Romani people, homosexuals, dissidents, the disabled, and everyone not aligning themselves with its ideology.

Testimonies from one of the largest death camps in Poland started to reach the public eye in 1944. A year later, representatives were invited to San Francisco to draw up the founding Charter of the United Nations. A Jewish correspondent in the Red Army, Vasily Grossman, was one of the first to document what had happened at Treblinka—how even trained dogs would not obey the Nazi soldiers on the death walk to the gas chambers. "Children were able to breathe for a longer time than the grown-ups,"[1] he writes.

What had happened was such an industry of systematic horror that, to restore any faith in humankind, the inclination to attempt to move on from the devastating facts and images, rather than to remember what human beings are capable of, must have been strong.

The survivors testified to facts that are too terrible to grasp—the number of millions dead and human actions too vicious to understand. The Red Army, when reaching the death camps, confronted villagers who had lived only kilometers away from the enormous genocide that had taken place, forcing them to see what had occurred close to their homes, demanding them to acknowledge the dreads. Hitler's plan had been to rid the camps of all traces and keep thousands of witnesses to the genocide silent, but what had happened could not be buried.

After the Second World War, nations on the victorious side declared themselves to stand united and to act early on any future signs of governments turning against their people, which had so forcefully eroded the ethical principles of human equality and dignity. Equality and dignity were not won by victory in war; the respect for the ethical principles had to be regained through international deliberations, law-making, and politics based on human rights. The genocide had occurred in the middle of Europe, within industrial complexes—still the world had not reacted.

> Inhabitants of the village of Wólka, the one closest to Treblinka, tell that sometimes the screams of women who were being killed were so terrible that the whole village would lose their heads and rush into the forest, in order to escape from these shrill screams that carried through tree trunks, the sky and the earth.[2]

In that moment, as the Nuremberg trials with endless testimonies began in 1945, there emerged a willingness to compromise national interests for a greater global cause. This led the governments to declare a need for an international organization that would be given the mandate by its collaborative existence to limit national sovereignty in the name of peace and human rights. The delegates at the San Francisco Conference (United Nations Conference on International Organization, UNIO) proclaimed that there was such a thing as human rights and that it was the United Nations' core mission to protect these rights. "We the peoples of the United Nations determined to reaffirm faith in fundamental human rights, in the dignity and worth of the human person, in the equal rights of men and women and of nations large and small." This, the second paragraph of the preamble in the Charter, states the core of what would become the most controversial issues during both the San Francisco Conference and the drafting of the Universal Declaration of Human Rights. The controversy began when the fundamental principles of equality and dignity were discussed in terms of women, children, minorities, and people under colonial rule. That men and women were equal was not a belief held by all delegates. That both large and small nations would have a say in international diplomacy was not evident. Finally, that the dignity of the human person included 'everyone' without distinction was still to be debated in listing grounds for discrimination.

This book is partly a story of the origin of the United Nations, the Charter and the Declaration drafting, but primarily a story of the unknown women who sat at the table.

## Notes

1. Vasily Grossman, *A Writer at War: Vasily Grossman with the Red Army 1941–1945*, ed. Antony Beevor and Luba Vinogradova (London: The Harvill Press, n.d.), 296.
2. Ibid.

# Acknowledgments

Credit to the UN Dag Hammarskjöld Library, the UN Archives, and the UN Photo Library. Quotes from UN Record Meetings have been changed from past to present tense. Images from UN Photo have been reproduced with permission of UN Photo © UN Photo.

Quotes from Virginia Gildersleeve, *Many A Good Crusade: Memoirs* (1954) reproduced with permission of Simon and Schuster © Simon and Schuster. Quotes from Begum Shaista Suhrawardy Ikramullah, *From Purdah to Parliament* (1998; originally published 1963) reproduced with permission of Oxford University Press, Pakistan © Oxford University Press. Credit to the Dominican Republic, publisher of *Lucha y Agonía* by Minerva Bernardino (1993). Quotes from *Lucha y Agonia* used in the book have been translated from Spanish to English. Credit to Australasian Book Society, publisher of *Truth and Repose* by Jessie Street (1996). Credit to Butala & Company, publisher of *Indian Woman* by Hansa Mehta (1981), efforts have been made to contact the publisher.

Credit to the Franklin D Roosevelt Library archives. Credit to the Sigtuna Foundation clip-archives. Quotes from Swedish archival newspapers articles from 1945 to 1948 used in the book have been translated from Swedish to English.

Thanks to the Swedish-American Foundation for funding the Women of the Declaration project in 2014, together with the Swedish Fulbright Commission.

Jake Shifman for editing the whole manuscript. Molly Edlundh, Felicia Granath, Paulina Troillet Mancini, Jonna Mannberg, Annika Ullman, Joakim Landahl, Klas Roth, and Frida Hagström for feedback on chapter drafts. My students in the 2015 cohort class on 'Women and Human Rights' and Marco Helles at *Enskilda Högskolan Stockholm* University College Stockholm, Stockholm School of Human Rights for encouragement and inspiration.

# Introduction

## A Counter Narrative to Earlier Research

The Universal Declaration of Human Rights has been philosophically linked to earlier declarations such as the French Declaration of the Rights of Man and of the Citizen 1789 and the Bill of Rights of the United States of America 1791. Partly due to this historicizing, a number of postmodern scholars argue that human rights must be reclaimed and rearticulated, taking into account non-Western cultural and religious values, with the presumption that these conflict with 'human rights' as they have been conceived. This historicization bases 'human rights' on a discourse of individualism and as incompatible with collective notions of morals and ethics.

Chantal Mouffe, for one, criticizes the way that a Western notion of human rights has been universalized and forced upon non-Western societies. Should resistance and conflicts surprise us? she rhetorically asks.[1]

However, as earlier historical accounts have demonstrated, it was not only Western delegations in the United Nations bodies that debated the Declaration; at the establishment of the United Nations in 1945, only fourteen out of fifty-six Member States to the United Nations were European.

### The Drafters of the Declaration?

Earlier research on the drafting process, which led to the adoption of the Universal Declaration of Human Rights in 1948, has generally emphasized the contributions of the Western and male delegates who participated in that process.[2] The French delegate to the Commission on Human Rights, René Cassin—who was also a member of the Drafting Committee—has long been viewed as the 'father' of the Declaration.[3] Johannes Morsink[4] has challenged this view by highlighting instead the contribution of Canadian delegate John Humphrey, who collected eighteen drafts of international bills of rights before the first meeting of the Commission on Human Rights. Supplementary to these descriptions, Mary Ann Glendon[5] offers a special weight on Eleanor Roosevelt's influence in the Commission on Human Rights alongside male delegates Charles Malik from Lebanon and Peng Chang from China.

While Jay Winter,[6] Paul Gordon Lauren,[7] and Morsink[8] draw out historical narratives emphasizing the influence of Western male delegates on the initial drafts of the Declaration and Glendon[9] adds historical accounts of the intellectual influence that non-Western male delegates such as Malik and Chang had on the Declaration alongside female Western delegate Eleanor Roosevelt, this book offers a competing historical narrative of the debates that included non-Western female delegates who made the Declaration inclusive of women by advocating for 'human rights' rather than the 'Rights of Man.' The United States representative Eleanor Roosevelt is the only female representative who has been given substantial attention in earlier research on the historical narrative of the creation of 'human rights' at the United Nations.

Hillary Charlesworth, feminist law scholar, has criticized 'human rights' for pertaining to men's rights:

> Because the law-making institutions of the international legal order have always been, and continue to be, dominated by men, international human rights law has developed to reflect the experiences of men and largely to exclude those of women, rendering suspect the claims of the objectivity and universality of international human rights law. Until the gendered nature of the human rights system itself is recognized and transformed, no real progress for women can be achieved.[10]

In her research, Charlesworth points to the fact that women were a minority in leading positions within the United Nations. Indeed, when we acknowledge how slowly the process of appointing female delegates to different high positions in the United Nations has unfolded, the prevalence of the role that women played at the outset is rather surprising.

In Europe, the political roles that women played during the Second World War to combat the Nazi occupation in the postwar years were not recognized for their political significance. For example, French women involved in the resistance movement against the Nazi occupation did not receive the same acknowledgment as their male counterparts.[11] Only six women received recognition for their resistance through *Le Croix de la Libération* after the Second World War—four out of the six being awarded posthumously—in contrast to over a thousand men who received *Le Croix*.[12]

Were there other neglected parts of women's history in the postwar years? In researching women's role at the creation of the United Nations, there were thrilling findings to be revealed at the United Nations Archives at the Dag Hammarskjöld Library in New York. In the minutes from the sessions in which the Universal Declaration of Human Rights had been voted through, there appeared new female delegates whose names were not mentioned in earlier research on the drafting. This turned out to be another neglected part of women's history—the narrative of female delegates to the United Nations in 1945–48.

Why was it that at that time in history that there were several prominent women taking part in international negotiations between countries in the United Nations? Their achievement—to place the notion of gender equality in the United Nations' initial documents—is even more noteworthy as in many countries women had only recently been eligible to participate in public politics.

This story is a partial one, chosen to unveil parts of history yet untold. The drafting process was a struggle for equity in a war-ridden world scourged by conflicts between different political, economic, religious, and cultural value systems. The female delegates' proposals and arguments were colored by their experiences: of claiming women's rights beyond religious divides; a Muslim female delegate's battle against the political and economic oppression of women; and a Hindu female delegate's non-violent struggle against colonialism for independence and recognition of rights, a Dominican female delegate's advocacy for women's place in politics; and a Polish female delegate's insistence that no one forget the displaced, the refugees, or the stateless people. In joining their voices, they forged a new accord. This was not to be a replication of United States' Bill of Rights (1791) or of the French Declaration of the Rights of Man and of the Citizen (1789). This was not another white-male-privileged list of rights but a counter narrative, thus another fragment forming women's history. [13]

Within feminist research, creating counter narratives is seen as a political act; that is, using hegemonic stories to create counter narratives by unearthing alternative sequences, experiences, and trajectories.[14] As stories of women's political influence in history continue to be overshadowed by an endless reification of maleness and whiteness, there is a shortage of narratives to which women can relate their experiences—especially non-Western women. Who is regarded as a political subject with an active voice of agency becomes limited to the repertoire of historically represented subjectivities.[15]

The significant involvement of women in the creation of human rights that this book highlights can be explained in part by the fact that the Universal Declaration of Human Rights was drafted after two world wars when women had advanced their political positions in joint struggles with men for peace and independence. Some of these female representatives to the United Nations had played significant roles in the movement toward the independence of their states.

Member States such as India and Pakistan were progressive regarding female representation in the postwar years. In most European countries, women had formally gained their right to vote and become eligible for political positions in the late nineteenth and early twentieth century, but many countries in Europe still had not allowed women a place in politics. Member State Switzerland was one of the last countries to grant women the right to vote in the 1970s—twenty years after both Pakistan and India had outstanding female Muslim and Hindu representatives in their delegations to the United Nations to draft the Universal Declaration of Human Rights.

In light of the minimal attention paid the female contributors to the drafting of the Declaration in earlier research, there remain insights to be gained by acknowledging alternative narratives. Considering these perspectives entails questioning the static quality of rights in terms of both universality and particularity. From this inquiry into the drafting of the Declaration where counter narratives contest the reification of a European male subject, we can illuminate the broader point that notions of political subjectivity are able to morph through the availability of additional or competing historical narratives.

Reading the Declaration through narratives other than the Western narrative of the origin of human rights enriches human rights studies as arguments for human rights put forth in 1948 by the female delegates from India, Pakistan, and the Dominican Republic, grounded in their different religious and cultural values, contain important messages about the document.

Although women played a significant role in the movement toward independence in India and Pakistan in 1947,[16] historical accounts have focused mostly on Mahatma Gandhi as the leader of the Indian Independence movement and on Muhammad Ali Jinnah as the founder of Pakistan, but there were many courageous women who walked with them. Though there were women involved in the drafting of the first constitutions of India and Pakistan—two of whom were also part of drafting the Declaration, Hansa Mehta (India) and Begum Shaista Ikramullah (Pakistan)—their roles have been subsequently overshadowed by male, nationalist narratives in the retelling of their historical founding.

In the following chapters are some of the women who have not shared equal acknowledgment in historical research on the drafting of the UN Charter and the Universal Declaration of Human Rights: female representatives who debated the UN Charter in Committee II and III at the San Francisco Conference, and the Declaration in the Commission on Human Rights, the Commission on the Status of Women, the Humanitarian, Social, and Cultural Third Committee, and the General Assembly.

From a feminist perspective, the counter narratives of non-Western female politicians, researchers, writers, educators, lawyers, and diplomats who affirmed human rights on religious and divergent ideological grounds—often the same religious beliefs that today are conflated on an international scale with a rejection of women's human rights—raise questions of the power to define belonging. Who has historically had the right to claim human rights, in which contexts, and on what ideological grounds? There is a need to question the social and gendered boundaries prevailing in answers to such questions.

Due to the marginalization of these non-Western women's voices through earlier recounting of the creation of human rights in the United Nations, scholars have argued that conceptions of human rights reflect the concerns and freedoms of a male, universal subject that neglects the lived realities and challenges of women. According to Judith Butler,[17] the definition of 'human' and thus of human rights represents a universalization of man and of male subjectivity. Therefore, the basis of human rights rests on a notion of a human dignity that fails to include women, children, 'minorities,' or 'anyone other' than a white, male subject.

Butler argues that there exists a dichotomy between the intended international legitimacy of human rights and the dominant local notion of human rights as Western. In Butler's view, there is a need for cultural translation as a method of re-reading human rights through occasionally conflicting cultural and religious value systems to create a more inclusive notion of rights, or a limited list of rights and freedoms that would be acceptable in divergent moral value systems.

Butler's critique is solid when and if we presume that the dominant Western, male narrative on the creation of human rights is unquestionable. In my earlier writings,[18] I have focused on what I referred to as an 'intersectional dialogue' surrounding the United Nations debates on the universality of human rights, precisely to question this Eurocentric narrative that I argue is additionally reified through its postmodern and feminist critiques of the universality of human rights.[19]

In 1946–48, as the Declaration was debated and finally adopted, delegations from different nations defended the universality of human rights based on Catholic, Christian, Islamic, and Hindu religious beliefs as well as on liberal, socialist, communist, secular, and feminist beliefs about social justice. They did not agree on a 'right' basis for human rights, but they agreed on a list of rights to accommodate conflicting ideological grounds. For this agreement to be reached, delegations held over 200 sessions—debates that led to an abstraction of the text—as specific cultural and religious references had to be deleted from the document. This is the reason why there is no mention in the Declaration of any conception of 'God' as the basis for human dignity, nor to specific discriminatory practices such as apartheid, the caste system, or racial segregation.

Within any dominant narrative that gives precedence to one description of what it means to be human over another, there are the untold, the silenced, the marginalized stories—the counter narratives that disrupt the reified notions of the dominant narrative. There is a political dimension of particular narratives[20] that shouldn't be ignored in favor of a totally relativistic position which criticizes identity politics of social categories. Particular narratives can be used as a means of highlighting violations of social justice from groups' perspectives of oppression of marginalized peoples. However, too much faith in the particular to represent 'all' marginalized within a specific group has been heavily criticized in feminist research that problematizes 'women' as a homogenous entity. This is a critique of white privilege blindness in feminist research that overlooks how different social structures other than gender create marginalization. Whenever people meet in a political context, not one but multiple categories of positional power relations are at play that can effectively silence communication. These include, but are not limited to, social status, race, class, gender, sexuality, language, nationality, ethnicity, and age.

This book aims to introduce neglected voices and open new venues for future research on human rights. How can voice and representation be understood in relation to women's history in the aftermath of the social crisis that led to the drafting of the Declaration? Most of these historical female delegates came from privileged social and economic classes; did their rights struggle for political, social, and economic rights neglect or abandon the needs of women from other classes and social backgrounds in their countries?

Were they sensitive to the ways in which patriarchal structures of economic and political disparities between women and men suppress women in vulnerable situations even more harshly? Or must we assert, as does Gayatri Spivak[21] through the notion of the subaltern (those who have no political voice), that, as soon as one gains access to the educated bourgeoisie, claiming representation of the speechless is a form of colonial practice far from speaking of justice in solidarity with the oppressed?

When encountering the names of all these women in the United Nations Archives, I was initially wary of not focusing on representation but on political action. The women of the Declaration influenced the wording; they vouched for inclusion. They are not silent names; they created a new narrative—of human rights as inclusive of women. The story of these women focuses on those delegates who had a say in different United Nations bodies throughout the drafting of the UN Charter and the Universal Declaration of Human Rights. There were many noteworthy women in these settings, behind the scenes, worthy of their own stories to be told—but this story unfolds as the two founding documents of human rights in the United Nations took shape. It is a counter narrative of women in the history of the United Nations from 1945 to 1948.

The UN Charter reaffirmed in its preamble equality of men and women, thanks to persistent argumentation of Latin American women delegates. The Universal Declaration of Human Rights went through different United Nations' bodies; ultimately, seven drafts of the Declaration were debated and amended through this process. Article 1 of the Declaration began in the first draft: "All *men* are born free and equal in dignity and rights. They are endowed by nature with reason and conscience, and should act towards one another like *brothers*." When the Declaration had come through the Third Committee to be voted on in the General Assembly, Article 1 read: "All *human beings* are born equal in dignity and rights. They are endowed with reason and conscience and should act towards one another *in a spirit of brotherhood*."[22]

## Notes

1. Mouffe, Chantal. (2005). *On The Political*. London: Routledge
2. Michael Ignatieff, *Human Rights as Politics and Idolatry* (Princeton NJ: Princeton University Press, 2003); Lynn Hunt, *Inventing Human Rights: A History* (New York: W.W. Norton & Co., 2007).

3. Jay Winter, *Dreams of Peace and Freedom: Utopian Moments in the 20th Century* (London: Yale University Press, 2006).
4. Johannes Morsink, *The Universal Declaration of Human Rights: Origins, Drafting, and Intent*, Pennsylvania Studies in Human Rights, 99-1997995-3 (Philadelphia, PA: University of Pennsylvania Press, 1999).
5. Mary Ann Glendon, *A World Made New: Eleanor Roosevelt and the Universal Declaration of Human Rights* (New York: Random House, 2001).
6. Winter, *Dreams of Peace and Freedom.*
7. Paul Gordon Lauren, *The Evolution of International Human Rights: Visions Seen*, Pennsylvania Studies in Human Rights (Philadelphia, PA: University of Pennsylvania Press, 2003).
8. Morsink, *The Universal Declaration of Human Rights.*
9. Glendon, *A World Made New.*
10. Hilary Charlesworth, *Human Rights: Critical Concepts in Political Science* (London: Routledge, 2008), 135.
11. Claire Duchen, *Women's Rights and Women's Lives in France 1944–1968* (London: New York: Routledge, 1994).
12. Ibid., 136–81.
13. See further Rebecca Adami, "Intersectional Dialogue—Analyzing Power in Reaching a Universal Declaration of Human Rights in 1948 on Conflicting Grounds," *Journal of Human Rights* (August 25, 2017); Rebecca Adami, "Intersectional Dialogue—A Cosmopolitical Dialogue of Ethics," *Cosmopolitan Civil Societies: An Interdisciplinary Journal* 5, no. 2 (August 14, 2013): 45–62; Rebecca Adami, "Reconciling Universality and Particularity Through a Cosmopolitan Outlook on Human Rights," *Cosmopolitan Civil Societies: An Interdisciplinary Journal* 4, no. 2 (August 27, 2012): 22–37.
14. Rebecca Adami, "Counter Narratives as Political Contestation: Universality, Particularity and Uniqueness," *The Equal Rights Review* 15 (2015): 13–24.
15. Ibid., 15.
16. Aparna Basu and Bharati Ray, *Women's Struggle: A History of the All India Women's Conference 1927–1990* (New Delhi: Manohar Publications, 1990); Geraldine Forbes, *The New Cambridge History of India. Women in Modern India* (New York: Cambridge University Press, 1996); Vrinda Narain, *Reclaiming the Nation: Muslim Women and the Law in India* (Toronto, Buffalo, London: University of Toronto Press, 2008).
17. Judith Butler, "Contingent Foundations: Feminism and the Question of 'Postmodernism'," in *Feminist Contestations: A Philosophical Exchange*, ed. Seyla Benhabib et al. (New York: Routledge, 1995), 35–58.
18. Rebecca Adami, *Cosmopolitan Civil Societies.*
19. Fiona Webster, "The Politics of Sex and Gender: Benhabib and Butler Debate Subjectivity," *Hypatia: Journal of Feminist Philosophy* 15, no. 1 (2000): 1–22; Seyla Benhabib, "Subjectivity, Historiography, and Politics," in *Feminist Contestations: A Philosophical Exchange*, ed. Seyla Benhabib et al. (New York: Routledge, 1995), 107–26.
20. Particular narratives refer here to culturally, socially, and contextually articulated beliefs and ideas in the form of local discourses that frame social categorizations and moral conduct.
21. Gayatri Chakravorty Spivak, "Subaltern Studies: Deconstructing Historiography," in *Selected Subaltern Studies* (New York, Oxford: Oxford University Press, 1988), 3–32.
22. International Bill of Human Rights, December 10, 1948, A/RES/217(III).

# 1 The San Francisco Conference
## A Call to All Women

> [T]he word 'man,' although it is assumed that it represents all human beings, only represents its gender. On the other hand, it is evident that the term 'human' represents more the human race than the male gender. Here is why, in an instrument that transcends and in the value of the charter of rights, the male gender cannot represent the entire species.[1]
>
> —Minerva Bernardino, the Dominican Republic

### Controversies at the San Francisco Conference, 25 April 1945–26 June 1945

Before the San Francisco Conference in 1945, *Dagens Nyheter*[2] reported from New York that major hindrances toward the creation of the United Nations remained to be solved by the five Great Powers (the United States, the United Kingdom, France, China, and the Soviet Union). There was a plan in place to hold a two-week-long meeting in Washington before April 25th to solve these issues regarding how the votes would be divided in the Security Council, how to deal with the pressure from the Soviet Union for a Lublin-Committee to represent Poland in San Francisco, and whether Argentina would be given an invitation to join the San Francisco Conference.

The Soviet Union declared Argentina a fascist state and threatened that if Argentina were invited then Poland should be represented with the Lublin-Committee. The Lublin-Committee was a provisional government established by the Soviet Union in opposition to the Polish government that was still in exile in London after the Polish territory was retaken from Nazi Germany. This was against the Atlantic Charter that Stalin had signed at the Yalta Conference declaring that democratic elections would be held in countries controlled by the Red Army.

The Polish Government-in-Exile would send members in an unofficial capacity, as would the Lublin-Committee. Argentina was finally admitted to the Conference after pressure from the United States.

What seemed an irresolvable conflict between the Great Powers was the proposal from the Unites States for international trusteeship by the United

Nations of German colonies in Africa and Oceania. At the Peace Conference in Paris in 1919 after the First World War, it had been decided between the victorious powers that the colonies of Germany, Austria-Hungary, and the Ottoman Empire would be governed by the League of Nations themselves. Now both Britain and France wanted to take over the colonies. Instead of becoming autonomous, the colonies had come under the rule of the winning powers, who had divided these territories amongst themselves. Controversially, at the San Francisco Conference, the United States suggested forming Trustee Commissions in the United Nations that would be responsible for 'developing' these territories in such a way that they could eventually gain independence. This was met with resistance from United Kingdom and France, who wished to tie these territories ever more tightly to the existing colonial system. A compromise was met: Some colonies were divided between the winning powers, and some came under trusteeship of the United Nations.

The mandates had been divided into three different types, depending on the 'societal and cultural advancement' of the population of the colony relative to the population of the colonial empires. Class-A mandates were occupied provinces of the former Ottoman Empire, including today's Palestine, Iraq, Syria, and Lebanon. The populations of these lands were viewed by the Great Powers as 'sufficiently developed' after the First World War for active participation in the administration of their own territory in the near future. Iraq, nonetheless, won its independence from Britain in 1922 after a popular revolt, whereas Syria and Lebanon remained under French rule until 1947. The Class-B mandates included the German colonies in Africa, where the population of the colony would manage political control of their own territories in the 'foreseeable future.' Cameroon and Togo were divided between France and England. The Class-C mandates were sparsely populated territories in Oceania, which the powers decided were to be incorporated under the mandate of Australia and Japan.

The Americans desired a form of trusteeship in that an international Trustee Commission would be set up by the United Nations to regularly visit the mandates and present reports on their 'status.' The United States hoped to gain support for their position from Russia and China but would initially avoid openly mentioning the colonies and mandates of Italy and Japan, both sensitive subjects at the time.

The United Kingdom wanted to postpone the San Francisco Conference, but Franklin Roosevelt was convinced that the earlier the San Francisco Conference was held the better. An international organization for peace would gain greater support from the public before the end of the war as people were still living under the "fresh impressions of the current catastrophe."[3] The Conference would begin in late April 1945.

On 7 May 1945, German High Command would sign an unconditional surrender of all German forces. The triumph by the Allies was followed by the report six days later of the death of Franklin Roosevelt: "He was his own Foreign Minister and decided over United States foreign politics."[4] Delegates and advisors at the Conference, well prepared to work out a Charter, were suddenly forced to improvise in international politics, giving consideration to "relations with the British Empire, the Soviet Union, the American Republics and the Far East."[5]

Before the San Francisco Conference, there was diplomatic pressure from Egypt to reach a balance between the Great Powers and the other states. It was a way to keep international peace, according to the Egypt Foreign Minister Abdel Badawi.[6] In order not to produce a privileged position of the 'Great Powers,' a power balance within the new organization had to be created—something that had not been established at Dumbarton Oaks.

The overarching focus on issues covered by worldwide media from the San Francisco Conference concerned the undemocratic structure of the Security Council, perceived as the most influential force in maintaining world peace in the new organization.[7] At the San Francisco Conference, Norway had proposed that smaller states should have the opportunity to question a veto placed in the Security Council so that no nation would be forced into a solution that would hinder its future security and development. This proposal was voted down.

After this, the Soviet Union, initially in favor of the structure in the Security Council—where the Soviet Union was one of five permanent members with veto-power—turned its back on the negotiations and threatened to leave the Conference. Would the Security Council be given the authority to investigate conflicts in cases where one of the veto states wished to use their veto against such an intrusion on national sovereignty?[8] The Soviet Union claimed national sovereignty and veto-right above international cooperation against aggressions. The veto question, on how influential the veto-powers would be in the United Nations, threatened to erode cooperation and collapse the entire San Francisco Conference.

As the delegations continued their work on the United Nations Founding Charter, the Soviet Union expressed to the media that the Conference was unproductive.[9] The veto question was solved, after all, on 9 June 1945, less than three weeks before the end of the Conference. The Soviet Union agreed that a veto from one of the five Great Powers could only be laid when action that might inflict on national sovereignty was decided within the Security Council but not at the initiation of an investigation of an international conflict.[10]

The next problem on the agenda that received international media coverage was the issue of the mandates. The Soviet Union canvassed here for their immediate right to independence, but the United States and Great Britain wanted developments in these territories to be "in accordance with the will of the people."[11]

Questioning the continuing existence of colonies meant threatening the economic and political supremacy of the Great Powers in the global world, eventually leading to the Cold War where the influence over colonial and trustee territories was fought along Western liberal and Eastern socialist ideological lines.

Reports from the San Francisco Conference on 12 May 1945 stated that the way the Trusteeship Commission would be controlled by the international organization was an unresolved problem. Great Britain seemed close to giving its support to the American proposal that territory suitable as military bases would be controlled solely by the governments that would administer the bases.

The United States wanted undisputed control of some Pacific bases and for a while objected to independence as a goal for trusteed peoples.[12] The issue of the mandates in relation to claims for independence was not resolved at the San Francisco Conference but lingered on in the newly established United Nations bodies working in 1946–48 with the drafting of an international Bill of Rights. The question remained an overarching and unresolved controversy: Would the bill include people living under colonial rule?

The influence over the agenda at the San Francisco Conference showcased in many ways where the countries' alliances had lain during the Second World War. Evidently, Germany and Japan were not represented. Ukraine and the Byelorussian Soviet Socialist state were invited, even though their independence from the Soviet Union was questioned by Western states.

Other countries, such as Italy, were not invited to the Conference due to their stances during the Second World War. Denmark became the fiftieth member of the United Nations 7 June 1945 and was thereupon welcomed to participate in the last days of the Conference.[13] Sweden was initially not invited to San Francisco, until information surfaced in the media that Sweden had secretly smuggled weapons to Denmark to fight the Nazis.[14] On 13 June 1945, ten days before the Conference ended, Swedish newspapers reported that three new Member States might be invited to the San Francisco Conference: Poland, Italy, and Sweden.

At the end of the San Francisco Conference, the Economic and Social Council (ECOSOC) was created, viewed by experts as "maybe more important than the Security Council to prevent future wars," as experts had underlined how the "causes of war are economic rivalry, social conflicts and hindered necessary access to important raw materials."[15] The Swedish journals even went so far as to suggest that if the Economic and Social Council did its work according to its mandate, then it would eventually reduce the Security Council as an appendage of only historical interest but without any remaining functions:

> The reason for this optimism lies in the fact that the Economic and Social Council will deal with the foundational reasons for war and work for fair play in world trade, a maximum of production and employment, free exchange of information and unhindered international exchange of people, money, material and ideas.[16]

Had the Economic and Social Council succeeded in creating these economic and social justice changes through its international mandate, they would have—according to Swedish journals in 1945—lay the conditions for lasting international peace. Since the mandate of the Security Council was based on the veto powers to intervene when acts of aggression or other threats to world peace had already occurred, its functions would decrease when the preventive conditions of economic and social justice were established.

In hindsight, this view seems very idealistic as the present-day Security Council has become the most prestigious and powerful UN body for international politics and negotiations, whereas the operative work of the Economic and Social Council to prevent future aggressions and international conflicts has not gained as central weight in the United Nations organization.

## Stand Up for World Peace

The Charter of the United Nations was signed 25 June 1945. There would, with the new international organization, be an international security council, a general assembly, an economic and social council, an international court, and a permanent international secretariat. The Swedish journals reported "25 June 1945 will in history stand as the new world peace organization's birthday, the day when the new world Charter was formally signed by the fifty represented nations in San Francisco."[17] The historical moment occurred at eight minutes to eleven PM Pacific Ocean-time in the illuminated War Memorial Opera House adorned with the fifty national flags.[18]

The adoption ensued as the British ambassador to the United States, Lord Halifax, Chair at the plenary session, called the delegates approving the Charter to stand up from the benches instead of only raising their hands, as was customary. When the representatives to the United Nations solemnly rose from their seats, the hundreds of pressmen and the audience in the stands followed their example and waited under tense silence as the general secretary of the Conference, Alger Hiss, counted.[19] The auditorium held over three thousand people.

China was the first delegation to sign as the first nation to have been invaded by the axis. After China came the Soviet Union, with their memories from Stalingrad, the barricades in Moscow, and the Red Army that broke the German power on land. Next came the United Kingdom for their determination against the Nazi bombings. Then France, who had been defeated by and later (1944) freed from Nazi rule.

Mr. Koo painted his name with Chinese signs on the historical document with a bamboo pencil. This was the most widespread alliance seen at that point in history, with one hundred fifty signatory delegates who followed in this ceremony that lasted past midnight and took several hours. It follows that the signing date of the Charter has become referred to as 26 June 1945. Argentina, who would have signed first according to alphabetical order, came after the four permanent members of the Security Council, and the United States decided to place their signature on the Charter last.

The President of the United States held a reception that afternoon for all the delegations while the American Secretary of State held a dinner for the President at night, with only the Americans in attendance—a breach of international diplomatic etiquette, according to the single female delegate to the American delegation.[20] There had been four Member States chairing the sessions, but only one of them was invited to the dinner with the American President in San Francisco after the conference. "How can we expect other nations to like, to respect, and to cooperate with us if we treat them so rudely and are so absorbed in ourselves?"[21] she asks in her memoirs.

The day after the Charter was acclaimed, France asked for the "issue of Syria and Lebanon"[22] to be investigated by the United Nations, but that request was declined as the United Nations was not yet ready to address such problems. Syria and Lebanon gained their own independence from France a year later and would send their representatives to the United Nations in 1946.

In a journal article in a Swedish newspaper on the 27 June 1945, male delegate Smuts, former Prime Minister of South Africa, was described as one of the most influential figures at the conference in San Francisco.[23] Mr. Smuts was a general and representative of a country where the majority of the population did not enjoy the right to vote and controlled less than ten percent of the land, still he presented a first draft of the preamble to the UN Charter as including the wording 'human rights.' Were the founding documents for the new international organization not seen by all Member States as initially threatening national sovereignty or interfering with domestic politics of the time, either in South African racial laws or in the racial segregation in the United States?

Mr. Smuts didn't consider the veto issue that had dragged out the conference as problematic since, according to him, the great nations would be the ones upholding international peace and for this they needed the veto in the Security Council to pair their great responsibility with commensurate power.

Washington ambassador Mr. Halifax, President of the plenary session that acclaimed the Charter, announced "in the true meaning of the word we are a union of brothers who work on a common cause."[24]

There were sisters in the union too, yet the four female signatories to the Conference were not given notice by media as the South African male delegate received attention for his proposal to the preamble of the charter. It would take another year until the press reported on the effects of the mentioning in the Charter of equal rights of women, non-discrimination due to sex, and equal representation of women within the United Nations. At the signing of the Charter and in reports from the San Francisco Conference in June 1945, the influence by female delegates passed practically unmentioned.

*Figure 1.1* Virginia Gildersleeve speaks at a luncheon in her honor at the Mark Hopkins Hotel by the women of San Francisco on 26 May 1945.

Credit: UN Photo/Lundquist.

## Virginia Gildersleeve

In the American delegation to the San Francisco Conference, there was one female delegate, Virginia Gildersleeve, Dean at the Barnard College, an all-female college in New York.

Before the appointment as the only woman in the United States delegation Virginia Gildersleeve has crystalized her efforts on an academic career at Columbia University, where she earned a master in Medieval History. For a few years, she taught English part time at Barnard but turned down an offer for a full-time position to earn a doctorate in English and comparative literature.

After Virginia Gildersleeve received her doctorate, she was appointed to a lectureship in English at Barnard and Columbia. Two years later, she was made Associate Professor and, after one additional year, Dean at Barnard. In her memoirs, *Many a Good Crusade*, she calls to mind:

> The College was born because women in New York City wanted higher education. The Trustees of Columbia were unwilling to admit them

> to classes with the men in Columbia College, but said that if some public-spirited citizens wished to start a separate college for women and undertook to pay its cost, then they would guarantee the quality of instruction given in it and award the Columbia degree to its graduates.[25]

She felt this was a great acknowledgment and compromise for such a conservative institution.

Together with Caroline Spurgeon and Rose Sidgwick from England, they formed an International Federation of University Women (the Federation would later gain consultative status at the United Nations to the Commission on the Status of Women).

When Virginia Gildersleeve is asked by President Franklin D. Roosevelt to be representative of the American delegation to the San Francisco Conference, she has been Dean at Barnard for many years – a position she still holds in 1945. As Dean, she actively creates possibilities for her female students to continue their studies at the graduate level at Columbia University by hiring teachers in American politics. She wants her students to be able to pursue academic careers by offering subjects that female students can continue studying at Columbia, such as journalism. Through her position as Dean, she strategically builds on broader social engagement of alliances for peace across national borders with academics fleeing a war-torn Europe, generating a stimulating academic environment for her female students. This strategy provides her with the power to appoint highly regarded academics who otherwise might not have accepted positions at a female college. Margret Mead, who studies at Barnard in the postwar years, becomes a successful student of Franz Boas. Boas is professor in Anthropology, who opposed American involvement in the First World War as a German Jewish Socialist.

As Dean, Virginia Gildersleeve encourages both students and employees at Barnard to engage in the political movement for peace and justice. This is something not approved by the Barnard College Board of Trustees, who do not find it appropriate for young female students to demonstrate politically in the streets. The administration expresses the opinion that political activism is not 'ladylike' and is "too sordid for a refined woman."[26] Virginia Gildersleeve writes in her memoirs:

> I remember that in the first year of my Deanship the mother of one of our leading seniors came to me and implored me to prevent our students from marching in the Suffrage Parade. She said that to march in a parade would be a shocking and shameful thing for them to do and would injure the College greatly.[27]

Barnard is at this time one of six sister colleges, but education for women is seen merely as a refinement suitable for marriage. Virginia Gildersleeve questions this view through her Deanship in several ways. For example, she observes that male colleagues at Columbia University are able to take a year off from their positions with full salary for sick leave, but female colleagues who get pregnant are expected to drop their academic ambitions or find ways to be economically supported by their spouses. She enacts a maternity policy that provides one term off at full pay, or a year off at half pay, for all female faculty. Even though she herself never has children, many of her initiatives enable young women to combine continued studies with motherhood, which is rather progressive in the postwar years.

Even so, Virginia Gildersleeve is criticized by progressive feminists at this time for not recruiting enough female applicants for higher positions at Barnard, as professorships are dominated by men. She responds to this critique in her memoirs by explaining:

> We seemed sure to have plenty of women in any event, as the unusually competent ones in the lower grades were promoted to professorial rank. Therefore, when we were bringing in a new professor or associate professor, we were likely to try to bring in a man. Perhaps that was discrimination against women, but it was, I am sure, for the good of the college as a whole.[28]

She thinks that women should be assessed only in terms of equal qualifications. From her Deanship years at Barnard, she receives a high reputation amongst male colleagues, who confide in her stable character. She is the sole female in meetings at the Columbia Advisory Committee:

> Incidentally, from this inside view I learned another thing—that men and women are far more alike than is generally supposed, and that men frequently share equally traits attributed especially to women, such as jealously, a fondness for gossip, and an intensity of emotion.[29]

In her memoirs, Virginia Gildersleeve writes a chapter entitled "The Advancement of Women," in which she recalls that:

> It required patient months to win the confidence of male colleagues. Meanwhile, the militant feminists outside sometimes accused me of feebleness or indifference or treason against 'our cause.' In one sense perhaps they were right, for I would always, I think, have placed the welfare of the whole institution above the present advancement of our sex.[30]

The tactic that Virginia Gildersleeve pursues through her leadership in a male-dominated academic environment is one of patient listening and keeping a calm, poised character to win over the initial skepticism of her male colleagues. She reminisces:

> Most of my male colleagues outside Barnard had to be handled rather gently. Men were opposed to letting women in some courses and

> professional schools largely because they thought the women would cause trouble, would probably weep and faint at inconvenient moments, expect special consideration and privileges, perhaps lower the standards, and in general be a nuisance. I find that instead of arguing the principles of such matters with men, it is best whenever possible just to get a first-rate woman slipped in as unobtrusively as may be and then let her show that she is not troublesome and that she can do work as sound as the men students and perhaps better.[31]

This mindset of tactically winning over the approval of male colleagues to pursue agendas jointly might have led to some of her bewilderment when Virginia Gildersleeve encounters an opposite approach held by several other women delegates from Latin America at the San Francisco Conference.

In San Francisco, Virginia Gildersleeve meets Latin American feminists who will speak at as great a length as the male delegates and whose demands for the acknowledgment for women's rights is not an appreciated demand by male delegates. In 1945, Franklin D. Roosevelt appoints Virginia Gildersleeve as the only woman to the American delegation in San Francisco, a conference in which fifty state delegations will jointly draft a Charter of the United Nations. At the San Francisco Conference—where equality of women is for the first time mentioned in an international document through the Charter—there will be only eight female delegates. Only eight out of forty-six Member States have female delegates in their delegations, which equals eight out of eight hundred and fifty delegates. A total of three thousand five hundred people gathered at the San Francisco Conference, including advisors and secretaries. Less than one percent are women, even if women represent half of the population in every country.

## Acknowledgments

Quotes from *Many a Good Crusade* by Virginia C. Gildersleeve, copyright © 1954 by Virginia C. Gildersleeve; copyright renewed 1982 by Donald Vail, reprinted with the permission of Scribner, a division of Simon & Schuster, Inc. All rights reserved.

## Notes

1. Minerva Bernardino, *Lucha, Agonía y Esperanza: Trayectoria Triunfal de Mi Vida* (Santo Domingo: Republica Dominicana, 1993), 111–12. Intervention of Minerva Bernardino, delegate to the Dominican Republic at the sixth general assembly the United Nations. Theme: change of term from 'the Rights of Man' to "human rights" in the Universal Declaration and in the Charter. Third Committee, Paris, France, January 1952.
2. "Medlingsmöte i Washington för San Franciscokonferensen" [Mediation-Meeting in Washington Before the San Francisco Conference] by Thorsten Jonsson, correspondent, *Dagens Nyheter*, New York, April 3, 1945.
3. Ibid.

4. "Roosevelts död rubbade San Francisco-jämnvikten" [The Death of Roosevelt Shifts the Balance in San Francisco] by Walter Lippmann, *Stockholms Tidningen*, San Francisco, May 13, 1945.
5. Ibid.
6. Abdelfattah Badawi, *Peace for a Better World: Inspired from Egyptian Revolution* (USA: Xlibris Corporation, 2011), 15.
7. "Norskt förslag om småstaterna röstades omkull i San Francisco" [Norwegian Suggestion on the Small States Was Voted Down in San Francisco] by Thorsten Jonsson, *Dagens Nyheter*, New York, May 26, 1945.
8. "Sovjet ensamt i vetofrågan mot alla andra nationer" [Soviet Alone in the Veto Question Against All Other Nations] by Thorsten Jonsson, *Dagens Nyheter*, June 4, 1945; "Sovjets hållning i San Francisco är förbryllande" [The Soviet Position Confusing in San Francisco] by John Chester, *Stockholms Tidningen*, June 4, 1945; "Sovjet vägrar vika en tum i vetorättsfrågan" [Soviet Does Not Move an Inch in the Veto Question] by Ove Casparsson, *Aftonbladet*, London, June 4, 1945.
9. "Friscomötet till ingen nytta" [Franciscomeeting to No Use] by Isvestija, *Stockholms Tidningen*, June 5, 1945.
10. "Stalin gav med sig, Truman orubbligt fast i vetofrågan" [Stalin Gave in, Truman Stands Firm in the Veto Question], *Svenska Dagbladet*, June 9, 1945.
11. "Nästa tvist i San Francisco: frågan om mandaten" [Next Issue in San Francisco: The Question About the Mandates], *Göteborgs Handels- & Sjöfartstidning*, June 9, 1945.
12. "San Francisco: Interim Report. The Conference Is Making Progress, Though Not Toward Collective Security," Editorial, *Life*, June 11, 1945.
13. "Danmark som Nummer 50 blandt Nationerne i San Francisco" [Denmark as Number 50 of the Nations in San Francisco], *Kristeligt Dagblad*, Denmark, June 7, 1945.
14. "Sveriges aktier stiger i Frisco" [Sweden's Shares Rise in Francisco], *Handelstidningen*, June 13, 1945.
15. "Ekonomiskt och socialt råd viktigare än säkerhetsrådet" [Economic and Social Council More Important Than the Security Council], *Stockholms-Tidningen*, June 13, 1945.
16. Ibid.
17. "Det nya världsförbundet" [The New World Organisation], *Morgon-Tidningen/Social-Demokraten*, June 26, 1945.
18. "150 namn bekräftar San Franciscochartan" [150 Names Recognize the San Francisco-charter], *Stockholms-Tidningen*, June 27, 1946.
19. Ibid.
20. Virginia Gildersleeve, *Many a Good Crusade: Memoirs* (New York: Macmillan, 1954), 356.
21. Ibid.
22. "Franska förslaget om Syrien förkastades i San Francisco" [The French Proposal on Syria Rejected in San Francisco], *Svenska Dagbladet*, June 26, 1945.
23. "Den nya världschartan" [The New World Charter], *Associated Press*, June 27, 1945.
24. "Världsfred" [World Peace], *Dagens Nyheter*, June 27, 1945.
25. Gildersleeve, *Many a Good Crusade*, 67.
26. Rosalind Rosenberg, "Virginia Gildersleeve: Opening the Gates", *Columbia Magazine: The Magazine of Columbia University*, Summer 2001 Issue, 'Living Legacies' Series.
27. Ibid., 71.
28. Ibid., 79.
29. Ibid., 92.
30. Ibid., 98.
31. Ibid., 97.

# 2 A Charter Signed by Women?

> To retain the term, the 'Rights of Man' . . . would threaten the great achievements that women have reached in the field of rights. Indeed, we are sure that many countries would produce a pitiful confusion that would be detrimental to the dignity of the female sex and their aspirations towards a fair and total equality.[1]
>
> —Minerva Bernardino, the Dominican Republic

In many countries around the world, the first generation of women allowed to gain a university degree have become politically engaged in independence movements, peace movements, suffrage movements, and workers' unions. The social and economic hardships following two World Wars must be met with political struggles for a better future for a war-torn generation of children around the world. Women, organized through international suffrage movements, create a strong lobby at the San Francisco Conference to make the traditional notion of the 'Rights of Man' inclusive of women.

Of special concern to women's rights activists at the San Francisco Conference in 1945 is the preamble of the Charter, as well as Article 1 and Article 8. The preamble today reads as follows: "to reaffirm faith in fundamental human rights, in the dignity and worth of the human person, in the equal rights of *men and women* and of nations large and small."[2] Article 1 reads: "To achieve international co-operation in solving international problems of an economic, social, cultural, or humanitarian character, and in promoting and encouraging respect for *human rights* and for fundamental freedoms for *all without distinction as to race, sex*, language, or religion."[3] Article 8 reads: "The United Nations shall place no restrictions on the eligibility of *men and women* to participate in any capacity and under conditions of *equality* in its principal and subsidiary organs."[4] These wordings were of no small significance.

Four women will sign the UN Charter: Minerva Bernardino, the Dominican Republic; Wu Yi-fang, China; Bertha Lutz, Brazil; and Virginia Gildersleeve, the United States. Minerva Bernardino is Chair of the Inter-American Commission of Women. Wu Yi-fang is Principal of one of the

*Figure 2.1* Minerva Bernardino signing the UN Charter, Veterans' War Memorial Building, 26 June 1945 at the San Francisco Conference.

Credit: UN Photo/McLain.

most renowned female colleges in China. Bertha Lutz is a Brazilian delegate to the Pan-American Feminist Movement. Virginia Gildersleeve is Dean of Barnard College in New York and the only female politician in Franklin D. Roosevelt's presidential campaign.

At the Conference, there are eight female delegates in total. Four of the eight are signatories, in addition, there is Jessie Street, Australia; Åse Gruda

Skard, Norway; Cora Taylor Casselman, Canada; and Isabel P. de Vidal, Uruguay. Jessie Street is a feminist activist, journalist, and writer from Australia. Isabel P. de Vidal is Uruguay's delegate to the Inter-American Commission of Women. Åse Gruda Skard is an Assistant Professor in child psychology who establishes a national *Barnombudsman* (a representative for the rights of the Child) in Norway. She must leave the conference early to give birth to her fifth child. Cora Taylor Casselman is the fourth woman ever to serve in House of Commons in Canada, representing the district of Edmonton East. She also must depart early from the conference—a conference that will last for two months.

Apart from the four women signatories and the additional four female delegates, there are several female advisors and experts present at the conference. A prominent female advisor in the Mexican delegation is Amalia de Castillo Ledón; she is Vice-Chair of the Inter-American Commission of Women. Mexico has two female advisors in their delegation; as well as Amalia de Castillo Ledón, there is Adela Formoso de Obregón Santacilia, founder of the *Universidad Feminina de México*. There are two female counselors in the delegation from Venezuela: Lucila L. de Pérez Diaz and Isabel Sánchez de Urdaneta, member of the Pan-American Union who will be representing Venezuela at the drafting of the Universal Declaration of Human Rights a year after the UN Charter is signed.

## Latin American Feminist Agenda

Over the next two months, the delegations to the United Nations will collectively revise the statutory text that had been prepared at the Dumbarton Oaks Conference in October 1944. There are over eight hundred delegates present, and the work on the UN Charter lays the foundation for an international union whose main task is to promote peace through diplomacy between its Member States.

There are several important issues on the agenda. Among them: How will the Security Council be composed given its mandate to act in situations that may threaten world peace? Which commissions are needed under the Economic and Social Council to act for human rights in the world?

To facilitate discussions about each constituent clause of the Charter, twelve committees under four commissions are appointed, all with a representative from each delegation to work with lawyers on the wording of the text. A council of fourteen representatives will also be appointed, with an overall responsibility of coordinating the work of the various commissions and committees. Not a single woman delegate takes part in the Coordinating Council. Nonetheless, there is a strong women's rights lobby at the conference. Women's rights organizations have sent representatives to the conference to lobby for women's rights, and they create a parallel process to that of the main conference whereby a visionary agenda is set: 1) that non-discrimination applies regardless of sex, ethnicity, class, or religion; 2) to express explicitly in the preamble 'men and women'; 3) to state in the

Charter that positions in the United Nations should be equal for women and men; and 4) to create a full commission under the Economic and Social Council on women's rights.

In this parallel lobby process for the inclusion of an explicit mention of women in the Charter, the Latin American delegates Bertha Lutz, Minerva Bernardino, and Isabel P. de Vidal participate in their individual capacities as Chair, Vice-Chair, and delegate to the Inter-American Commission of Women. The two North American delegates, Virginia Gildersleeve and Cora Taylor Casselman, are not included in these discussions. Neither is the delegate of China, Wu Yi-fang, although she is positively observing the women's lobby.

Among the eight female delegates present at the conference, three camps are crystallized: the representatives from Brazil (Bertha Lutz), the Dominican Republic (Minerva Bernardino), and Uruguay (Isabel P. de Vidal) create an intimate and powerful Latin American feminist alliance supported by Australia's consultant (Jessie Street). The two North American delegates from the United States (Virginia Gildersleeve) and Canada (Cora Taylor Casselman) share the view that women's rights are implicitly included in the 'Rights of Man' and they want to work with the male delegates on equal terms without explicitly mentioning gender equality. The delegate of China, Wu Yi-fang, is supported by Norway's representative Åse Gruda Skard, both of whom pursue a rather low-key stance, standing behind the Latin American feminist alliance, although they do not pursue any questions themselves and maintain a moderate position not to support proposals they consider to be radically feminist.

Virginia Gildersleeve recalls in her memoirs:

> It was a great surprise to me when I found at San Francisco among some of the women delegates that old militant feminism which I thought had passed away. Some of the women felt it necessary to call attention frequently to women and their problems and to rub in the fact that they were women.[5]

The British advisors at the conference, Florence Horsbrugh and Ellen Wilkinson, share Virginia Gildersleeve's attitude. In England, women have already, during the first half of the twentieth century, achieved a certain amount of formal equality and, accordingly, they feel there are no urgent reasons for female representatives to 'behave like women.' When Florence Horsbrugh and Ellen Wilkinson arrive at the San Francisco Conference, they are met by enthusiastic reporters who want to hear from the conference's 'female delegates.' The two Brits respond with indignation, "We are *not* 'women delegates.' We are delegates of our country as ministers in our government."[6] The North American and British representatives want to stress the fact that they are there only on the basis of expertise, not necessarily representing women's issues. Virginia Gildersleeve sees women as "equal comrades with men working for the same end and on the same basis,"[7] although she is well aware that part of the reason she had been appointed was because she is a woman. When women's organizations attempt to contact female members in the British and North American delegations, they decline such cooperation, while the Latin Americans accept this invitation by the women's lobby, as does Jessie Street.

Jessie Street later looks back in her biography *Truth or Repose*:

> I was visited by members of women's organizations, some I already knew a few of them from our League of Nations work. Some of them had attended the Dumbarton Oaks meetings where the draft Charter had been prepared. They told me they had managed to have sex discrimination added to the Article [1] prohibiting 'any discrimination by Member Nations on the grounds of race, language or religion.' They also wanted the support of the Australian delegation for this wording and for a more specific Article [8] in the Charter establishing the right of women to hold any office in all the organs of the proposed United Nations Organization.[8]

*Figure 2.2* Minerva Bernardino, President, Inter-American Commission of Women and delegate of the Dominican Republic. Meeting of Committee III, 6 June 1945 at the San Francisco Conference.

Credit: UN Photo/Rosenberg.

According to Virginia Gildersleeve:

> There was really not very much for the militant feminists to do. The position of women so far as the Charter was concerned was definitely established by the words which occur often in various Articles: 'Human rights and fundamental freedoms for all, without distinction as to race, sex, language, or religion.' The inclusion of these words in the Charter was among the recommendations sent in before the Conference actually opened and sent in, oddly enough, by the Soviet Union.[9]

The Soviet Union had eleven full delegates in their delegation, but no women.

## Minerva Bernardino and Non-discrimination

Minerva Bernardino reflects years later on her experiences from the conference:

> The greatest opponents to the inclusion of women in the Charter were those from the two countries where women are most advanced, the United States and Great Britain, a 'paradox' attributable to 'domestic' battles over the Equal Rights Amendment proposed to the United States Constitution. Unfortunately, this problem of yours is also a handicap for women of the backward countries.[10]

The Equal Rights Amendment (ERA) to the United States Constitution had been proposed to insert prohibition of discrimination based on prejudice against sex; the Constitution already forbade discrimination due to race, color, religion, or national origin. The strong opposition to the Equal Rights Amendment was postulated on the need for protection of female workers. The argument was that equal rights would mean less protection for women in industry. Forty-three national organizations openly opposed the Equal Rights Amendment in the United States, including the American Association of University Women that Virginia Gildersleeve founded.

Minerva Bernardino will hold a special role in the enforcement of women's rights, both during the drafting of the UN Charter and later at the drafting of the Universal Declaration of Human Rights. There are two main accounts of her life and deeds—her own memoirs, *Lucha, Agonia y Espranza* (1993), where she lists her achievements and rise to political power in her home country and abroad—and a more skeptical account, "The Strange Case of Minerva Bernardino,"[11] that explores the contradiction in how she could fight politically for women's right to vote during a period of dictatorship in the Dominican Republic.

Both narratives are partial. On one hand, her life narrative is not exclusively built on personal achievements, as there are prominent women through whose association Minerva Bernardino gains broader recognition.

On the other hand, she is not merely diplomatic and ready to please political powers nationally and internationally—she has her own agenda to forward and takes on several battles in the United Nations for what she believes. Her strength is based on strong rhetorical abilities in her advocacy of women's rights combined with her ability to form alliances across national borders with other women from Latin American countries as well as with North American female politicians.

Minerva Bernardino, in comparison to several of the other women participating at the drafting of the founding documents, comes from a relatively modest background. Born in a small village in the Dominican Republic in 1907, her parents died when she was only fifteen, so she decided to move to Santo Domingo to work. Minerva Bernardino is part of the first generation of Dominican *normalistas*—women who receive an education—and she has carved out a career in politics at the Department of Education and Agriculture. Minerva Bernardino later says that her motivation for a feminist struggle was sparked by a situation that may sound paradoxical as it was when she was appointed Minister within the Department.[12] The problem was that her salary stayed the same as before the promotion, as her employer matter-of-factly explained that a woman could not earn more than her male colleagues. She then joined *Acción Feminista*, a Dominican feminist club established in 1930, with the aim to change national legislation on women's and children's rights, specifically aimed at increasing the protection for mothers and working-class women, all under the banner of feminism. The women who participated were economically well off or, as Minerva Bernardino, earned their living through teaching, working in the industry, or other blue-collar work.

Minerva Bernardino worked in national politics in the Dominican Republic during the Trujillo regime but found a gateway to Washington through her engagement with the Inter-American Commission of Women (IACW) where she met the American politician Doris Stevens in whom she found a strong ally in lobbying women's rights internationally.

Doris Steven was the United States' National Women's Party leader—founder and Chair of Inter-American Commission of Women. Minerva Bernardino lived an independent life and did not marry; therefore, when she moved to Washington, she got by through part-time jobs. In her memoirs, she recounts how these first years in Washington, when she walked with her typewriter to and from work, were lonesome but that she really enjoyed it. Having moved all the way from a small village in the Dominican Republic to the capital of the United States, she seems to have enjoyed her freedom.[13]

Other Latin American activists in the Inter-American Commission of Women are either elite by birth or professional women, but Minerva Bernardino sustained herself through a job as a typist in the Library of Congress; for a while, she gave Spanish classes to diplomats' wives. From Washington, she still endorses some influence over national politics on women's rights in the Dominican Republic, but she never returns to the

Dominican Republic. She will instead invest her devotion for the rights of women at the Inter-American Commission of Women, where she meets several female representatives from other Latin American Member States, many of whom she collaborates with at the conference in San Francisco. In her memoirs, she explains that her continued interest in influencing national politics on issues on women's rights was because she had seen how legislation drafted under totalitarian regimes concerning rights and freedoms seldom were changed once democratic freedom was achieved. With this conviction, she managed once to convince Trujillo to invite the head of the Commission, Doris Stevens, to a meeting in the Dominican Republic, after which Trujillo accepted their suggestion to sign the Pan-American Women's Nationality Treaty adopted at Montevideo.[14]

Minerva Bernardino once wrote a letter to Trujillo on reforming the nation's constitution to include women's political rights. Women formally gained suffrage in 1942 in the Dominican Republic but, since oppositional parties were abolished, this suffrage became rather symbolic.

By 1943, Minerva Bernardino is President of the Inter-American Commission of Women, a position she holds when the United Nations is formed. The Inter-American Commission of Women is influential during the San

*Figure 2.3* Amalia de Castillo Ledón, Vice President of Inter-American Commission of Women, meeting of Committee III, 6 June 1945 at the San Francisco Conference.

Credit: UN Photo/Rosenberg.

Francisco Conference in contrast to European-based feminist organizations ravaged by the war.

The women's organizations keep urging that 'sex' should be included in the Charter in the clauses prohibiting discrimination on the basis of race, language, or religion. This is backed up by the delegations from India, Brazil, the Dominican Republic, Mexico, and Uruguay. The proposal is given at the beginning of the conference by the USSR and accepted by the other sponsoring powers. A sub-committee is established to draft the exact text on the clauses prohibiting discrimination, with delegates from Australia, Brazil, Belgium, Canada, Netherlands, Norway, the United States, and Uruguay. The only countries voting against the inclusion of sex in the non-discrimination list are Cuba and the United States, although the text is accepted by a majority vote of thirty-four to two, with the United Kingdom abstaining. Virginia Gildersleeve perceives this inclusion in the Charter as leaving the "militant feminists"[15] with nothing more to do during the Conference, but she is mistaken.

## Women's Rights Lobby

Virginia Gildersleeve's aim during the Conference in San Francisco is to strengthen the four freedoms that Franklin D. Roosevelt mentions in his famous speech on 6 January in 1945. In his State of the Union speech before Congress, Franklin D. Roosevelt proposes four fundamental freedoms for people all over the world: freedom of speech, freedom of worship, freedom from want, and freedom from fear. Virginia Gildersleeve sees the Charter as a promising safeguard for these freedoms internationally. During the San Francisco Conference, she is responsible for writing a draft under the Second Council, and she hopes that her contribution in the American delegation, with her "devout admiration for the perfect Preamble of the Constitution of the United States of America," is able to achieve something 'equally good' for the new world organization.[16]

Virginia Gildersleeve works hard in her delegation. Her tactics lay in close reading of the texts and proposing amendments that focus on word selection in different paragraphs. Her close attention to the language of the Charter seems to be to her disadvantage—especially in contrast to the more passionate speakers on women's rights from the Latin American delegations. Virginia Gildersleeve does not seem to vouch for any strategic vision in her amendments. Rather, she is frustrated by linguistic deficiencies and the text's lack of aesthetic beauty in an academic sense. While the Latin American female delegates, together with Australia, welcome the draft-preamble proposed by Mr. Smuts from South Africa at the beginning of the Conference in which 'equality of men and women' is affirmed, Virginia Gildersleeve is annoyed by the ill-chosen words in his text.

Virginia Gildersleeve does not create alliances with the feminist delegates, whom she finds brusque, nor with the lobby for women's rights. She does not see herself as a speaker for only women's rights but rather of 'the rights of men,' which includes everyone implicitly. Virginia Gildersleeve's opposition to the inclusion of the wording 'men and women' in the preamble of the Charter is not supported by the male delegates, who seem affected by the Latin American delegates' conviction of the importance of strengthening women's position and rights through the new organization. The Latin American female delegates share a vision and passion that is contagious.

*Figure 2.4* Bertha Lutz, delegate of Brazil, Committee II, 15 June 1945, at the San Francisco Conference.

Credit: UN Photo/Mili.

Another explanation of why Virginia Gildersleeve is not actively supported by male delegates in her rejection of a mention of the equality of women and men in the preamble that the feminist lobby pursues might have been that the male delegates did not, in the turbulent days of the conference, consider the wording endorsed by the Latin American Feminists as important as the power of the Security Council and the use of veto by the Great Five. Lack of support notwithstanding, Virginia Gildersleeve has leverage in her position as representative to the American delegation, which is comprised mainly of men and includes over one hundred and twenty people at the Conference.

In her memoirs, Virginia Gildersleeve describes how the American and British men are "bored and irritated by repeated and lengthy feminist speeches" [17] and how the male delegates "hated being lectured on the virtues and rights of women."[18] The suffrage of women in America and Britain, gained earlier but finally used in national elections in the 1920s, had been fought for by national and international women's organizations, of which some are present at the Conference. It is rather interesting that the most 'progressive' delegations relative to domestic women's rights are the most hostile to the Latin American feminist delegates. American delegation staff "bestowed on Dr. Lutz the nickname 'Lutzwaffe' as a humorous adaptation of the German Luftwaffe, which had been devastating Europe,"[19] Virginia Gildersleeve recalls. This can be taken as a sign that the Latin American feminist alliance was influential during the Conference as even the most powerful of nations felt that they had to diminish the female delegates' position by ridiculing them amongst themselves. Virginia Gildersleeve notes, however, that men from other nations felt differently, speaking "with admiration of the feminists, especially of Dr Lutz."[20]

## Bertha Lutz and Article 8

The next thing for the feminist Latin American alliance to promote, with the lobbying support of international women's organizations at the Conference, is the wording in Article 8—to make sure that women have equal right to participate in the work in the organs of the United Nations. The wording today reads: "The United Nations shall place no restrictions on the eligibility of men and women to participate in any capacity and under conditions of equality in its principal and subsidiary organs."[21] Bertha Lutz from Brazil proposes a motion to insert into Article 8 "that men and women should be equally eligible to participate."[22] Virginia Gildersleeve evokes Bertha Lutz's prominent role:

> The outstanding leader of the feminists was Dr. Bertha Lutz, a delegate from Brazil, a distinguished scientist in the field of biology, a former Congresswoman, and President of the Confederated Association of Women of Brazil. Early in the proceedings I invited her and the other

> women delegates who had already arrived to tea in my sitting room. It was then that I first heard Dr. Lutz declare herself as a militant feminist in favor of what seemed to me as segregation of women.[23]

At the Conference, Virginia Gildersleeve advises Bertha Lutz to not ask for too much regarding women's rights, as it would be a vulgar thing to do.[24] When the United Kingdom, the United States, and Cuba oppose Bertha Lutz's motion on women and men's equal eligibility to participate, she responds in a well-prepared speech at the debate:

> We worked to obtain rights for women in Brazil for twenty-five years, women in the United States worked for sixty years and women in Great Britain for seventy years. Why should women have had to do all this work if it was unnecessary? I think if you would look at the laws and declarations of most countries, you would see that every one of them, beginning with the Magna Carta down to the Declaration of Rights, the preamble to the American Constitution, etc., you would find that men have never found it unnecessary to make a statement of their rights. Why, then, should it be unnecessary to make a statement of the rights of women?[25]

Bertha Lutz aims her rhetoric at the Western female delegates, and her question points to the weakness in their argument that women should not ask for anything—men in most countries around the world have secured their rights through national legislation—why should women, who have now gained some political influence, hold other women back from claiming their rights?

She continues:

> We also know that it has always been held that women have been included in the general term 'men' throughout the centuries, and we also know that it has always resulted in the fact that women were precluded from taking part in public affairs. Now things have changed. I have noticed that during the last few years in the United Kingdom the King always addresses 'the men and women of this country.' The same phraseology is found in the speeches of the President of the United States. It is also developing right throughout the Latin American Republics.[26]

Things have changed. Women are addressed and included as citizens, they are gaining political rights—this change is worldwide—and Bertha Lutz does not want it to stop at the national level. Women should be addressed in the United Nations and in international politics, too.

Bertha Lutz has a wide-reaching international network from her political engagement for women's rights in Brazil as the representative of the Brazilian government to the Female International Council of the International Labour Organization (ILO) and founder of a national organization in Brazil for women's right to vote. Before she went into politics, Bertha Lutz studied biology and natural science at the Sorbonne University in Paris, France, later moving back to Brazil to form the League for Intellectual Emancipation of Women.

Equipped with experiences both from international lobbying on women's rights and a law degree, she has presented several suggestions at the Montevideo conference on women's equal right to work and is well acquainted with the art of argumentation. Bertha Lutz continues the struggle for women's rights through the Inter-American Commission of Women, where she meets Minerva Bernardino.

In 1935, Bertha Lutz had been elected to the national congress and became one of the first female 'Congressmen' in Brazil. One of the first things she promoted was the establishment of a committee that overlooked all legal proposals and political directives in the Congress and how these affected women's rights; the committee was called Statue of Women. When the dictator Getúlio Vargas seized power in Brazil in 1937, the parliamentarian work on national political projects for women's rights reached an abrupt end for Bertha Lutz, but her international career for women's rights continued. For six years, Bertha Lutz serves as Vice President for the Inter-American Commission of Women, which has been built up under the guidance of Minerva Bernardino.

Bertha Lutz and Minerva Bernardino share a strong sense of commitment and many years of political advocacy for women's rights in Latin America through national politics in Brazil and the Dominican Republic. Minerva Bernardino is convinced that their efforts for reforms and progressive legislation are not in vain. In her memoirs, Minerva Bernardino reminds us, "In those days, some countries did not have democracy and human rights were constrained, nonetheless we had to push for women's rights anyway. History has shown that legislation created during dictatorship has not been changed by democratic governments."[27]

The resolution of equal eligibility of women to participate in the organization creates in the Committee III "heated debate, and strong opposition from the United Kingdom, United States and Cuba,"[28] recalls Jessie Street. Virginia Gildersleeve of the United States announces that the resolution will have to be resubmitted. The feminist Latin American alliance is troubled and annoyed by this. At any rate, they re-open the debate on their initial proposal through Senator Isabel P. de Vidal from Uruguay.

The female representatives from Australia, Jessie Street; Brazil, Bertha Lutz; and Uruguay, Isabel P. de Vidal defend the proposal.[29] They argue that the inclusion of women in the text will allow for the recognition of women's contributions to peace.

The opponents of an explicit mention of women in Article 8—Cuba, the United Kingdom, and the United States[30]—argue that such an inclusion is

*Figure 2.5* Jessie Street, Australian representative to the Commission on the Status of Women, and Amalia de Castillo Ledón, Mexico.

Credit: UN Photo.

unnecessary since non-discrimination is already mentioned in Article 1 of the Charter and that it might be seen as 'undue interference in domestic affairs' of Member States to call for equal representation in the Secretariat. Member States should, according to this view, have the right to not appoint any female representatives to the United Nations if they wish to deny half of their populations the possibility of direct influence within the United Nations.

The United States and Cuba are the only delegations voting against mentioning equal rights for women to hold positions in the United Nations, with an abstention from the United Kingdom—and the resolution is voted through. Bertha Lutz, heading the Latin American feminists on this note, succeeds in having women mentioned in Article 8 of the Charter, declaring that women should be eligible without restrictions to hold positions in the United Nations.

## Setting Up a Commission on the Status of Women?

Will there be a commission with experts on the rights of women in the United Nations? Committee III is authorized to deal with the clauses of the UN Charter, to set up the Economic and Social Council, and to reach a decision on which additional commissions are needed. Virginia Gildersleeve feels Committee III is not as important as her meetings in the committee assigned with issues concerning the Security Council while Jessie Street sees Committee III as essential since the establishment of the Commission on the Status of Women is to be debated therein.

Jessie Street has been President of the Committee of the Feminist Club since 1928.[31] She knows the importance for women to collaborate in politics to be granted a space normally withheld from them. Creating a feminist space, in her experience, is for women as important for its 'social amenities'[32] as for its empowering effects. When Jessie Street attends Committee III, she is delighted to work with colleagues on a joint cause—"Among the other members I was glad to see our whole women delegates' liaison committee—Bertha Lutz, Minerva Bernardino, Amalia Ledón, Isabel Urdaneta, and Isabel Vidal—and they were just as pleased to see me."[33] The feminist alliance meets daily and lobbies the other members in Committee III, and Jessie Street feels that:

> Many of them recognized that women were regarded as second-class citizens in nearly every country and that a special campaign would have to be undertaken throughout the United Nations to ensure that women were accorded universal respect and that human rights and fundamental freedoms applied to them.[34]

In Australia, Jessie Street has campaigned for political parties to nominate women candidates for the Commonwealth Parliament in 1931 when she "found the selection process as closely guarded as any club of men."[35] Even though she had managed to gather a list of female candidates for the Commonwealth Parliament, all of them withdrew their candidature as their husbands individually had reached the conclusion that 'letting' his wife participate in politics would jeopardize his career.

National politics, like international politics, was, in Jessie Street's view, an exclusive Boys' Club; even if women were allowed entrance, there was a need for new strategies in order to make a visible difference—from mere representation at the lowest levels to occupying power positions at the highest. As husbands felt threatened by their wives' participation, men in politics felt threatened by women candidates:

> Women could join the party and do canvassing and organise meetings, distribute literature, send out notices and other work essential to winning an election, but no party wanted women candidates, particularly in a seat they had the slightest chance of winning.[36]

In the United Nations, one strategy was to create a commission exclusively for women to investigate the legal and political status of women internationally. The Latin American feminist delegates propose the establishment of a separate Commission on the Status of Women at the San Francisco Conference.

The Brazilian delegation, with Bertha Lutz, proposes this commission to study conditions and prepare reports on the political, civil, and economic status of women and their opportunities, with special reference to limitations placed upon them on account of their sex. Thirty-three delegations support a Commission on the Status of Women, but Virginia Gildersleeve, on behalf of the United States, and Wu Yi-fang, on behalf of China, oppose such a commission. In their view, a Commission on the Status of Women will segregate women and men and will therefore contravene the principle of non-discrimination. Wu Yi-fang and Virginia Gildersleeve do not find it necessary to mention women specifically in the Charter as they are understood to be included in the wording 'everyone.' They see it, rather, as an upcoming task of the Commission on Human Rights in the new organization to deal with the elimination of discrimination against women and other 'minorities.'

Jessie Street is the only Western woman delegate who supports this initiative. She expounds on the dispute in the Committee: "The argument that most human rights had been enjoyed exclusively by men and denied to women and that a single body would not address this was exhaustively debated, with the United Kingdom and the United States firmly opposed."[37] Reflecting back on her stance at the conference, Virginia Gildersleeve writes in her memoirs:

> Perhaps in the backward countries, where women have no vote and few rights of any kind, spectacular feminism may still be necessary. My English friend Caroline Spurgeon, with whom I lived so long, used to tell me that I did not appreciate the need of militant feminism because I had not been trampled upon enough. If I had lived my life in England in the old days, she told me, I would have been very different.[38]

Still, Virginia Gildersleeve concludes that she believes that women should not "talk much about the abstract principles of women's rights" and instead do a good job.[39]

But how were women supposed to do so if excluded from higher education, work opportunities, and high positions?

Virginia Gildersleeve of the United States opposes the creation of a Commission on the Status of Women for the same reasons she has opposed the Equal Rights Amendment—she thinks a Commission on Human Rights will be able to cover issues of women's rights and that separatist strategies militate against the notion of non-discrimination. Virginia Gildersleeve reminisces:

> There was so much talk about this matter of the Commission on the Status of Women that most of us got very tired of it, and some of the men especially were inclined to say, "Oh, let the women have their own commission and keep away from our meetings."[40]

Virginia Gildersleeve's argument against setting up a separate Commission on the Status of Women was that women's rights would be accounted for

*Figure 2.6* Wu Yi-fang, President of Ginling Women's College; Member of People's Political Council; delegate of China, Committee III, 6 June 1945 at the San Francisco Conference.

Credit: UN Photo/Rosenberg.

in the Commission on Human Rights: "Speaking on behalf of the United States, I opposed this, contending that women should be regarded as human beings as men were and that the Commission on Human Rights would adequately care for their interests."[41]

The proposal of a separate Commission on the Status of Women by Minerva Bernardino of the Dominican Republic is voted down, even though many delegations at the Conference support the initiative. There is still an opening to raise the question at a later stage since it is decided that new commissions can be created under the Economic and Social Council.[42]

## The Only Asian Woman to Sign the Charter

The fourth woman to sign the UN Charter in 1945 is Wu Yi-fang, delegate of China. Wu Yi-fang is part of a new generation of women who gain university degrees after the end of the Qing Dynasty. As are many of the other prominent female delegates at the San Francisco Conference, Wu Yi-fang is well educated; she earned a PhD in 1928 in biology and philosophy at the University of Michigan in the United States. Upon her return to China after her doctorate, she is appointed Principal at Ginling Women's College, a position she will hold for twenty-three years. Wu Yi-fang is one out of five Presidents of the People's Political Council. As one of few individuals to continue a political career during and after the Cultural Revolution, Wu Yi-fang will be appointed Vice President of Nanking Normal University, Director of the Bureau of Education for Jiangsu Province, first female Vice-Chair of the Jiangsu provincial government, and finally Vice President of the All-China Women's Federation.

Like Minerva Bernardino, Wu Yi-fang has worked hard and overcome many obstacles to reach the international conference in San Francisco. Minerva Bernardino and Wu Yi-fang have both experienced the loss of a parental safety net at a young age and the subsequent pressure of having to support themselves financially. As a teenager, Wu Yi-fang lost her father and her elder brother to suicide after the family business became bankrupt. Wu Yi-fang had to work during her studies to help her mother financially. Her opportunity for a future career and for the family's economic survival was a recommendation by an English teacher for her to continue studying at the Ginling Women's College.[43]

The motto for the Ginling Women's College is a rather apt description of Wu Yi-fang herself: "The purpose of life should not only be about yourself, but also about helping people and society with one's wisdom and ability. By doing so, it will not only benefit others, but also make one's life more rounded."[44] As Principal, Wu Yi-fang changes the regulations of her university from being a religious educational institution to making it accessible for students both with and without religious backgrounds.

Wu Yi-fang is the only Asian woman to sign the UN Charter in 1945 (China being represented by the Republic of China) at the San Francisco Conference.[45] As a delegate of China, Wu Yi-fang is a member of the sub-committee assigned the task of redrafting the adopted text of the Charter and the preamble that Virginia Gildersleeve does not favor. The draft of the preamble, which, to the delight of Bertha Lutz, Minerva Bernardino, Amalia Castillo de Ledón, and Jessie Street, has been adopted unanimously 'in principle,' Virginia Gildersleeve finds "far too long, ill arranged in part, and occasionally couched in clumsy, awkward English."[46] The sub-committee that will redraft the Charter includes representatives of Belgium, Chile, China, France, New Zealand, Panama, South Africa, the United Kingdom, the United States, and the Union of the Soviet Socialist Republic. Virginia Gildersleeve's suggestion is a revised version with only one hundred thirty-three words instead of the original two hundred. In her memoirs, she does not comment on her choice of wording, but the reference to women is being deleted. The wording 'equal rights of men and women' is changed in her proposal to 'equal rights of men,' but the committee will not delete 'women' in the second paragraph.

Numerous amendments to the preamble are proposed by different delegations, and Virginia Gildersleeve exclaims that she can't stand how the language is treated. A male delegate responds, "But, my dear lady, this is not literature. This is politics."[47] The text is not debated based on some literary pretense but negotiated between different vantages about this new world order. As another male delegate of the Soviet Socialist Republic, who passionately debates every word, has said earlier in the Conference: "Behind words is meaning. And behind meaning is life."[48] The final text of the preamble contains one hundred seventy-eight words, including 'the equal rights of men and women.' It is unanimously accepted by the committee and afterward by the commission and the plenary. After the vote in the committee, Virginia Gildersleeve hopes the Coordinating Council will alter the text of the preamble and 'smooth it out and throw it into a better form,' but this does not happen, something she says later that she looks back upon with sorrow.[49]

Jessie Street, however, leaves the Conference in higher spirits. For her, the work done by women's organizations and the feminist Latin American alliance is a hopeful sign for what may be possible, as she has not given up on the idea of a Commission on the Status of Women in the United Nations. While male politicians had, in her experience, been consumed by hunger for prestige, she felt that women endorsing change—as through her Feminist Club in Australia—had been more occupied with the necessities from the war of need and reconstruction. "[W]e tackled problems and took action to achieve our aims wherever possible."[50] "The same unity of purpose," she feels, "had been demonstrated on an international scale during these months in San Francisco."[51]

Today, the preamble of the UN Charter reads: "to reaffirm faith in fundamental human rights, in the dignity and worth of the human person, in the equal rights of men and women and of nations large and small."[52] Article 1 in the Charter lays out the purposes of the United Nations: "to achieve international co-operation in solving international problems of an economic, social, cultural, or humanitarian character, and in promoting and encouraging respect for human rights and for fundamental freedoms for all without distinction as to race, sex, language, or religion."[53] Lastly, Article 8 in the Charter states that the United Nations shall place "no restrictions on the eligibility of men and women to participate in any capacity and under conditions of equality in its principal and subsidiary organs."[54] The wording 'without distinction, as to sex' is repeated in Articles 13, 55, and 76 in the UN Charter.

## Acknowledgments

Quotes from *Many a Good Crusade* by Virginia C. Gildersleeve, copyright © 1954 by Virginia C. Gildersleeve; copyright renewed 1982 by Donald Vail, reprinted with the permission of Scribner, a division of Simon & Schuster, Inc. All rights reserved.

## Notes

1. Minerva Bernardino, *Lucha, Agonía y Esperanza*, 111–12. Intervention of Minerva Bernardino, delegate to the Dominican Republic at the sixth general assembly the United Nations. Theme: change of term from 'the Rights of Man' to "human rights" in the Universal Declaration and in the Charter. Third Committee, Paris, France, January 1952. (Transl. from Spanish to English by author).
2. The UN Charter, preamble.
3. Ibid., article 1.
4. Ibid., article 8.
5. Gildersleeve, *Many a Good Crusade*, 350.
6. Ibid., 349.
7. Ibid., 350.
8. Jessie M. G. Street, *Truth or Repose* (Sydney: Australasian Book Society, 1966), 180.
9. Gildersleeve, *Many a Good Crusade*, 351–52.
10. Ellen Carol Dubois and Katie Oliviero (eds.). (2009). "Special Issue on Circling the Globe: International Feminism Reconsidered, 1910 to 1975," *Women's Studies International Forum*, Vol. 32, Issue 1 (2009): 1–66. Page 48 (quoting Bernardino (1947), 4).
11. DuBois and Derby, "Special Issue on Circling the Globe."
12. Bernardino, "Introduction," in *Lucha, Agonía y Esperanza*, xxii.
13. DuBois and Derby, "Special Issue on Circling the Globe."
14. Ibid.
15. Gildersleeve, *Many a Good Crusade*, 351.
16. Ibid., 344.
17. Ibid., 352.
18. Ibid., 353.
19. Ibid., 353.
20. Ibid., 353.
21. The UN Charter, article 8.
22. Street, *Truth or Repose*, 182.
23. Gildersleeve, *Many a Good Crusade*, 350.
24. E. Dietrich Luhr, "Gender Equality—A Latin American Contribution to the Constitution of the World" (master thesis, Centre for International Studies and Diplomacy, SOAS University of London, 2016), 13.
25. Street, *Truth or Repose*, 182.
26. Ibid.
27. Bernardino, "Introduction," in *Lucha, Agonía y Esperanza*, xxviii.
28. Street, *Truth or Repose*, 182.
29. Ibid., 280–83.
30. United Nations Conference on International Organization (UNCIO), vol. VII: 31, 64.
31. Street, *Truth or Repose*, 67.
32. Ibid.
33. Ibid., 180.
34. Ibid., 182.
35. Ibid., 85.
36. Ibid., 85.
37. Ibid., 181.
38. Gildersleeve, *Many a Good Crusade*, 353.
39. Ibid.
40. Ibid., 352.
41. Ibid., 352.

42. The UN Charter, article 68: The Economic and Social Council shall set up commissions in economic and social fields and for the promotion of human rights, and such other commissions as may be required for the performance of its functions.
43. Zhejiag Provincial Archives. Personage's Scripts in Our Collections: Wu Yifang. http://www.zjda.gov.cn/archive/platformData/infoplat/pub/archivese_52/gcmrsj_2408/shouji-WuYifang2.html (23 May 2018).
44. Ibid. See further the Ginling College Records in the Smith College Archives.
45. The United Nations and most Western nations refused to recognize the People's Republic of China (PRC) during the Cold War until Resolution 2758 was passed by the General Assembly in 1971 and the PRC replaced the Republic of China representatives in the United Nations.
46. Gildersleeve, *Many a Good Crusade*, 344.
47. Ibid., 347.
48. Ibid., 334.
49. Ibid., 347.
50. Street, *Truth or Repose*, 186.
51. Ibid.
52. The UN Charter, preamble.
53. Ibid., article 1.
54. Ibid., article 8.

# 3 The United Nations 1946

## Will Women Have a Say?

> The fact that the Charter explicitly proclaims the equality of the sexes is a triumph for the women of the world. It is not an empty triumph; legislators in various countries are proceeding to implement those provisions of the Charter. Nevertheless, some States still have constitutions which grant rights, in particular suffrage, to men alone.[1]
>
> —Minerva Bernardino, the Dominican Republic

### A World in Need of Cooperation—Reconstruction and Peace

There existed an immense need for a new international organization that would work to reconstruct what the two World Wars had scattered and to create diplomatic foundations for lasting peace. When the Economic and Social Council met at Lake Success in New York in 1947, discussions centered on what to do about the issue of housing and the proliferation of slums throughout the world. In Warsaw, there were over 400,000 people living in holes dug out of the ruins. In Calcutta, workers lived in huts without sanitary systems; in the United States, thousands of soldiers lived in old railway carriages.[2] There was a widespread lack of industrial construction materials in many countries, as well as a lack of transportation infrastructure, which called for the initiation of cooperative international efforts. New methods to mass produce doors, windows, and piping had to be quickly spread across the world.[3] Belgium could export pipes, window glass, bricks, and steel. Switzerland could fabricate aluminum if they could get bauxite, while France had overflows of bauxite that was not used.[4] Poland could export coal if another country provided the transportation to move it. Sweden and Norway could provide the world with timber if coal and trucks were sent to mobilize it.[5] In merging the connections that allowed for the redistribution of supplies, there existed the possibility of reconstructing buildings and establishing new housing for families across Europe.

The focus for the international organization seemed mainly to have been reconstruction plans for a war-torn Europe. India and other countries that had experienced immense humanitarian suffering under colonial rule were not included in the relief program of the United Nations after the Second World War, as many 'governments' under foreign administration did not ask for such support. Perhaps this is because they were not representative of their people but of foreign interests of their colonial administrations?

The fourteen points that United States President Woodrow Wilson had laid out as imperative for world peace at the end of the First World War were at that time viewed by France, the United Kingdom, and Italy as naïve. In light of two World Wars, these points received greater weight as less idealistic and more reasonable. The fourteen points included covenants of peace to be achieved in view of the public, the sea outside territorial waters to be open for boat traffic, removal of economic barriers and the equality of trade conditions among all nations consenting to peace, that national armament be reduced to a minimum consistent with domestic safety, and that a general association of nations must be formed under specific treaties for territorial integrity of great and small states.

The first time *United Nations* was mentioned in an official document had been during the Second World War in the Atlantic Charter, a policy statement released by the United States and Great Britain and backed by twenty-six nations united against the Axis powers. The Atlantic Charter was a pledge to leave territorial borders unaltered, respecting the wishes of the people and pledging global cooperation for better economic and social conditions for all; to abandon the use of force; and to disarm aggressor nations. The vows made to self-determination and self-government would be challenged when political conflicts disrupted international diplomacy.

## Without a Permanent Headquarters

After the historical signing of the UN Charter on 25–26 June 1945, it will take another four months until all signing Member States have ratified the Charter. The signing will be a symbolic proclamation that the Member States stand behind the principles of the UN Charter. With the ratification of the document, the articles become legally binding for its members. Thus, it is not until the end of October 1945 when the United Nations is officially established.

The Opera Hall in San Francisco had been the perfect location to host the over two thousand participants at the conference proceedings, including journalists and international organizations, with its golden-lit main hall.

Where else would such a huge organization, comprising delegations from over fifty countries, convene? The international organization finds itself homeless in the first years of its existence—the same years when the Declaration is being drafted. As the future main headquarters in Manhattan, New York, is constructed—after a generous donation by the Rockefeller family—between 1946 and 1952, the United Nations will hold its sessions in other locations in London, New York, Geneva, and Paris.

## The Opening Session of the United Nations

The First General Assembly holds its opening session in January 1946 at the Central Hall Westminster in London, the capital's largest conference venue. It is a beautiful, freestanding, white stone building on the Thames, surrounded by a small park overlooking Big Ben—a spectacular site for the United Nations General Assembly inauguration. The place, with its white dome, marble staircase, and red velvet floor in the great hall that can welcome over two thousand people, must have contributed to the air of grandiosity of the events happening within. Trygve Lie of Norway is elected first Secretary-General of the United Nations, a post that he holds from February 1946 until he resigns in November 1952. Trygve Lie had been Chairman of the commission responsible for drafting the Security Council provisions of the Charter in San Francisco—another example of where the focus of the main figures had been during the Conference. He will hold this position until the tensions of the Cold War will lead to his resignation in 1952 and is thus Secretary-General during the years when the organization is drafting the Declaration, the years when the United Nations awaits a permanent headquarters.

The General Assembly Hall at the future headquarters in New York will have the capacity to seat around one thousand eight hundred people. The buildings in Manhattan will be designed by architects, planners, and engineers working as a multinational team to collaborate on the design (Australia, Belgium, Brazil Canada, China, France, Soviet Union, Sweden, United Kingdom, and Uruguay). The headquarters will also have a prayer room for all religions. Designing such a room for joint prayer was a rather difficult task since no faith-specific symbols were to be used but only what could speak to all people of faith. Unsurprisingly, the room became rather minimalistic in its final interior design.

In the wave of democratization—as royal empires in Europe have been scattered by the First World War and colonial powers have begun to lose terrain during the Second—women gain political terrain, but only a few have the education, influence, and economic means to participate in international politics.

At the first session of the United Nations General Assembly in 1946, seventeen women delegates to the General Assembly sign an 'Open Letter to the Women of the World'; amongst them is Eleanor Roosevelt, the United States; Marie-Hélène Lefaucheux, France; Minerva Bernardino, the Dominican Republic; Bodil Begtrup, Denmark; Ellen Wilkinson, Britain; Eydokia Uralova, the Byelorussian SSR; and Jeane McKenzie, New Zealand, who call upon women to take a more active role in politics and government. In this letter, they write:

> We hope their [women's] participation in the work of the United Nations Organization may grow and increase insight and in skill. To this end we

> call on the Governments of the world to encourage women everywhere to take a more active part in national and international affairs, and on women who are conscious of their opportunities to come forward and share in the work for peace and reconstruction as they did in war and resistance.[6]

They are all prominent political figures. The United Kingdom, hosting the inauguration in London, is represented by female delegate Ellen Wilkinson. She embodies this ideal of taking an active role in international and national politics in her work as a delegate to the United Nations and Minister of Education in England. Ellen Wilkinson works tirelessly the last years of her life, her health worn away by overwork, as she directs all her energy into the Education Act of 1944, which ends school fees and makes education a right even for the working-class children of England. After the Act is voted through British Parliament, she holds the position as Minister of Education from 3 August 1945 to 6 February 1947. During her two years as the British Minister of Education, she manages to also act as advisor to the British delegation in San Francisco and delegate at the opening session of the General Assembly in 1946. It will not be until the Declaration reaches the Third Committee of the General Assembly in 1948 that the United Kingdom will again be represented by a female delegate (Margery Corbett Ashby), as Ellen Wilkinson dies in office 6 February 1947.

## Placing Human Rights on the Agenda?

The question of placing human rights on the official agenda of the General Assembly is raised at its seventh meeting, four days after the opening session on 14 January in London. The delegation of Cuba raises this issue.

Mr. Dihigo points to the fact that the General Assembly of the United Nations will have to adopt a document to define the human rights mentioned in the Charter:

> As regards human rights . . . although the Charter establishes the general principles, it very wisely did not go into the details of what those rights are. It merely recognizes that human rights exist, and that these rights are likely to change in the course of time. It leaves to the Assembly the faculty of determining those rights, and that is what we have to do here.[7]

Several delegations object, fearing that to rush this pivotal issue will only result in conflicts over the definition of what human rights would encompass. What Cuba and other Member States will discover in this new international organization is the great amount of time necessitated for democratic processes in rooms of such diversity. Endless deliberation over the principles of 'human rights' will make this notion more inclusive than many of its members held that it would be at the San Francisco Conference when it was first mentioned in the Charter.

The Soviet delegations held that the 'Rights of Man' also included the rights of nations. Mr. Manuilsky of the Ukrainian Soviet Socialist Republic declares:

> I fear we shall encounter many difficulties if we attempt to discuss the subject now. There are many historical documents dealing with the Rights of Man. There is, for instance, the Magna Carta of English liberties. There is in France, the Declaration of the Rights of Man and of the Citizen. There is in the Soviet Union, the Declaration of the Rights of Nations of 1917, written by the great Head of our State, Stalin.[8]

The weight of these historical documents in shaping 'human rights' will be heavily debated in the United Nations. Female delegates from Southern countries will testify to the discriminatory interpretation of the 'Rights of Man' to which the documents from Soviet, France, and the United Kingdom refer.

The Cuban delegation wants to stress to the world that the General Assembly is placing human rights on its agenda:

> Jointly with the material help that we are going to send through the United Nations Relief and Rehabilitation Administration to those peoples that are starving, send also the spiritual message that, at the same time that we are sending them food and clothes, we are trying to set up the rules that will define the rights of men everywhere in the world.[9]

This suggestion is voted down in the General Assembly by a majority of delegations, and the Declaration is not placed as a special point in the agenda. Instead, the Economic and Social Council will establish commissions under its mandate explicated in the Charter to draft a Declaration of human rights that the General Assembly can consider at a later stage.

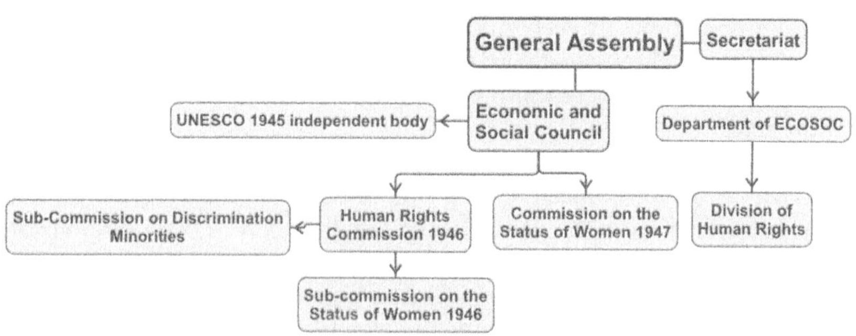


*Figure 3.1* Structure of the UN bodies mentioned as involved in the drafting of the Universal Declaration of Human Rights (UDHR).

## The Promising Mandate of the Economic and Social Council (ECOSOC)

It was not solely international politics that was under reconstruction with the establishment of the United Nations—Franklin Roosevelt had literally rearranged the list of speakers in the planning of the United Nations so that greater and smaller nations were mixed on the speakers list he prepared for the First General Assembly, though he did not live to see its opening session himself. This initial vision of a more democratically distributed influence would be challenged by the arrangement of the Security Council.

The Economic and Social Council and its eighteen members, under which many commissions will work, is more 'equal' than its brother, the Security Council. Decisions are reached by a simple majority, and no veto power exists. The members are chosen based on qualifications in the economic, cultural, or humanitarian area rather than by nationality.[10]

By June 1946, the Member States of the United Nations have already realized how democratic decisions made in the Economic and Social Council restrict national interests to use the United Nations as an extension to governmental agendas. 'The Russian group'—Russia, Ukraine, Czechoslovakia, and Yugoslavia—see their demands rejected in the Economic and Social Council.[11] They have demanded the International Work Union be accepted as a member of the UN and for the International Refugee Organization to start a hunt for war criminals and traitors amongst the 1.6 million refugees in Europe in the non-Russian occupation zones. The Russian group also wants a decree passed in the Economic and Social Council that the United Nations will limit the investigation to determine the reconstruction plans in the war-torn territories in Europe and Asia. All three demands are voted down by a majority of the council's eighteen members. Instead, the Council decides on a commission with twenty states that will be responsible for the investigations and drawing up a plan for reconstruction of the war-torn territories.[12]

## Will the New Organization Have Any Leverage?

The UN Charter states that the purpose of the organization is to work for peace and human rights. Therefore, the Commission on Human Rights will have the important task of comprising the views of Member States into one document listing the articles on human rights. The work of the Commission on Human Rights is not, however, given as much weight as other concerns in the new organization that seem more acute, such as how the Security Council is to respond to international aggressions and conflicts between states. Will the new organization lack the political leverage to influence Member States, as the preceding League of Nations had been powerless when Hitler seized power over the Ruhr area?

The League of Nations had failed its mission. While the organization had managed to collect over eleven million signatures for peace in Great Britain alone, it had not acted against the aggressions that led to the Second World War. Economic interests of the Great Powers had not been aligned with world peace, as Germany kept militarizing through imports from private enterprises in England. The victorious parties of the First World War had created an unsustainable situation by indebting a defeated country and by continuously exploiting coal from the Ruhr area while simultaneously selling material required for Germany's future aggressions.

As Jessie Street writes in her memoirs on the role of the League of Nations after the First World War:

> One big flaw in the postwar program was that nothing was being done to rehabilitate the German economy in the direction of production for peaceful purposes to deter German re-militarization. . . . The only people who had benefited were those with interests in the sale of raw materials for munitions and the munition makers themselves.[13]

Jessie Street's account partly contradicts the narrative of the United Kingdom and France's firm opposition to Germany, which claims that between the First and Second World Wars, Churchill defended peace and stability. Even though the League of Nations and the United Kingdom urged avoidance of confrontation in foreign political diplomacy, Jessie Street's description indicates that economic interests in both France and the United Kingdom—of continued trade with Germany even after it started upscaling for war—contributed to the Second World War:

> If the United Kingdom and France had wanted war with Germany and Italy they could not have acted more effectively. Added to this, reports circulated that large credits were being advanced to the Germans by interests in the British Commonwealth countries, in France and in the United States to buy war materials for making armaments. By the late 1930s, the manufacture and distribution of destructive armaments made war a looming threat, but in spite of the warnings and pleadings of the League of Nations Unions and the many affiliated international bodies, governments seemed unwilling or unable to control this nefarious traffic.[14]

Behind the corporations were private profiteers, reluctant to admit the connection between their own benefit and the dangers of a prospering war. "I remember the astonished reaction of my husband's uncle in 1930 in London," Jessie Street recalls, "when I pointed out the dangers to peace of selling nickel, the essential raw material in arms manufacture, to the Germans."[15]

## The Commission on Human Rights

The world's largest international organization is homeless, without a permanent headquarters in its early years of work. After its first January session in London, the United Nations moves to New York. From March through June 1946, the United Nations will use the Old Gymnasium Building of Hunter College north of Manhattan with large Gothic windows overlooking the waters of the Jerome Park Reservoir (present-day Lehman College). The campus was used during the Second World War as a training ground for women in the military.

By 29 April 1946, six commissions have had their first constitutional meetings at Hunter College in New York.[16] One commission will be dealing with human rights and the protection of minorities. The Commission on Human Rights, which initially seemed of less importance than the influential Security Council and the Economic and Social Council, draws attention as the International Bill of Rights gains global recognition as a 'Charter for Humanity.'

Several years after the creation of the Commission on Human Rights, Swedish diplomat and politician Agda Rössel states her opinion in a newspaper article after a visit to Geneva that "the Commission on Human Rights is much more interesting and in its work much more influential than one generally sees here at home."[17] She writes that, as an advisory expert organ with rather special tasks and limited powers, its foundation was directly connected to the United Nations' mission to establish something that could "become a kind of constitution for the whole of humanity."[18]

Agda Rössel describes many of the delegates in the Commission on Human Rights as anything but bureaucrats. She mentions Hansa Mehta, India; Mr. Cruz, Chile; and Mr. Malik, Lebanon as colorful delegates in the Commission on Human Rights. Their agenda was not solely to draft paragraphs of legal concerns, writes Agda Rössel, but to address human issues of injustice that were actualized in the discussions on the thirty articles of the Declaration. Among her insights from seeing the Commission at work, she explains that focus on specific wordings in the meetings led to interesting debates on fundamental issues of moral weight:

> A fact is that the Commission in its effort to find exact and at the same time general formulations were nearly often faced with the most immediate and most severe human realities. The disagreements were not just formalistic, but regarded basic concepts of vital issues.[19]

Agda Rössel describes how continuous discussions in the Commission on Human Rights were brought about by the definition on the right to work, in which the Eastern delegations, especially the Soviet Union, wanted to use formulations that indicated the responsibility of the state to provide 'mandatory work.' The expression would consequently include forced labor, which was not an opinion shared by other delegations. In this regard, as on many other wordings on rights and freedoms, fundamentally divergent ideological conceptions were conflicting, and it was the task of the experts in the Commission on Human Rights to frame the articles as clearly as possible to not fall into any ideological interests that might undermine worldwide acceptance of the list of rights.

*Figure 3.2* Minerva Bernardino, the Dominican Republic, and Xu Yizhen, China, members of the Sub-Commission on the Status of Women at a party given by Secretary-General Trygve Lie, 29 April 1946.

Credit: UN Photo.

## Is There Support for Human Rights among Divergent Ideological Contexts?

At the outset of drafting an international Bill of Rights, the United Nations' Educational, Scientific, and Cultural Organization (UNESCO) creates a parallel committee to the Commission on Human Rights drafting committee. The Committee on the Philosophical Principles of the Rights of Man carries out an inquiry into the theoretical problems raised by the elaboration of an International Declaration of the Rights of Man.[20] The Director of UNESCO, Mr. Huxley—who is responsible for creating this committee—in a correspondence with Mr. Havet, suggests that the 'Committee on the Philosophical Principles of the Rights of Man' be based in Europe to build its work primarily upon European thinkers and historical rights-trajectories. This suggestion is later questioned since the Bill of Rights is intended to be universal—so what philosophical and ideological foundation was there for a notion of the 'Rights of Man' in all societies, regardless of the divergence of moral and ideological systems?

To respond to this inquiry, thinkers and intellectuals from different parts of the world are invited to send letters based on a universal rights discourse in diverse cultural, religious, and ideological contexts. The report from UNESCO to the Commission on Human Rights will, in its final stage, include contributions on: "The Conception of the Rights of Man in the U.S.S.R. Based on Official Documents" by Boris Tchechko; "Human Rights in the Chinese Tradition" by Chung-Shu Lo; "The Rights of Man and the Islamic Tradition" by Humayun Kabir; "Human Freedoms and the Hindu Thinking" by S.V. Puntambekar; and "The Rights of Dependent Peoples" by Leonard Barnes, amongst many.[21]

The two female intellectuals invited to contribute by UNESCO's "Committee on the Philosophical Principles of the Rights of Man" are the Swedish writer and politician Alva Myrdal and former Secretary-General of the League for Penal Reform Margery Fry from Great Britain.

Alva Myrdal does not respond to the invitation but later travels to Geneva to participate at a United Nations meeting of the Economic and Social Council during the drafting of the Universal Declaration of Human Rights. Margery Fry, on the other hand, sends a written contribution entitled "Human Rights and the Prisoner," in which she discusses how the moral dignity of a society can be estimated by how the dignity and human rights of the prisoner is upheld. Her contribution speaks of the essential safeguard that human rights constitute: their hindrance of states from processes of dehumanization that may lead to human rights atrocities. Her contribution is an important critique of the international negligence to create a basic standard for the human rights of prisoners and an acute response to the dehumanization and illegalization through forced statelessness that had occurred during the Second World War.

The process of discussing these divergent contributions seems to have been an educational practice for those involved, and here UNESCO is really involved in their core aim: to enhance educational, scientific, and cultural communication of rights to promote peace and understanding amongst the Member States of the United Nations.

The list of rights that UNESCO's 'Committee on the Philosophical Principles of the Rights of Man' compiles will be, surprisingly, almost identical to the list of articles in the final Universal Declaration of Human Rights. As Jacques Maritain, Chair of the Committee, notes:

> [S]omeone expressed astonishment that certain champions of violently opposed ideologies had agreed on a list of those rights. 'Yes,' they said, 'we agree about the rights but on condition that no one asks us why.' That 'why' is where the argument begins.[22]

It is noteworthy that rights were discussed not only as legal entitlements but also in terms of practical principles to guide moral conduct between peoples and individuals. Mahatma Gandhi, who contributed a letter, mentions being inspired by his 'illiterate but wise mother'[23] to always talk about the duties people have toward others and that all rights have corresponding duties.

When parts of the report 'Human Rights—Comments and Interpretations,'[24] is published by the Weekly Bulletin of the United Nations in 1947, the Commission on Human Rights is still drafting the Declaration. A closed session is dedicated to discussing whether the report should be reproduced for distribution to all the Member States of the United Nations, as is common for all United Nations reports.[25] Since the report has not been an initiative by the Secretariat, this becomes an issue. The Commission decides not to distribute the report 'Human Rights—Comments and Interpretations' to all Member States. There were worries in the Commission on Human Rights that the report would be given uncalled-for attention. Work in other United Nations bodies would not, however, overshadow the immense effort made over several years by the delegates to the Commission on Human Rights in shaping the Declaration as we know it today.

## Will the Commission on Human Rights Cover Women's Rights?

There are eighteen delegates to the Commission on Human Rights: sixteen men and two women. The initial conflict between Virginia Gildersleeve of the United States and Bertha Lutz of Brazil on the creation of a Commission on the Status of Women at the San Francisco Conference in 1945 continues between the United States delegation and female delegates from Latin America at the outset of the work in the United Nations in 1946. United States delegate to the Nuclear Commission Eleanor Roosevelt opposes Minerva Bernardino's suggestion of setting up a Sub-Commission on the Status of Women under the Commission on Human Rights. She argues, in similar terms as Virginia Gildersleeve, that a Commission on Human Rights will adequately cover issues related to women's rights.

The Latin American feminist representatives continue their advocacy for '*la Comisión de la Condición Jurídica y Social de la Mujer*.' This title may better frame the mission in its explicit reference to examining and improving the 'legal and social condition' of women around the globe. Minerva Bernardino meets with Eleanor Roosevelt to explain their motivation, which is enhanced by the experiences at the San Francisco Conference, in which Eleanor Roosevelt had not participated. The male delegates to the Conference, Minerva Bernardino points out, had outnumbered the female delegates, and not all delegations saw it as evident that women were included in the traditional concept of the 'Rights of Man.' The Southern women delegates had succeeded in including the explicit mention of non-discrimination based on sex. This is an accomplishment that Minerva Bernardino wants enforced through the international document on human rights that is about to be outlined by a drafting committee in the Commission on Human Rights. It is most vital for Minerva Bernardino that a Sub-Commission is created on the Status of Women since men will not raise issues related to women's rights in the same way as a Commission of only women will.[26] Eleanor Roosevelt is not convinced of this.

Minerva Bernardino contacts Bodil Begtrup of Denmark about becoming the Chair of the Sub-Commission. "Acknowledging that as a delegate from dictator Trujillo's Dominican Republic, she could not become Chair," Bernardino explains that she would like to be Vice-Chair and that Angela Jurdak of Lebanon should be Rapporteur.[27]

Lacking due support from the United States delegation, Minerva Bernardino, Bodil Begtrup, and Angela Jurdak will lobby corroboration from other delegations, international organizations, and the New York Press for a separate sub-commission.

The Economic and Social Council decides to set up a Sub-Commission on the Status of Women under the Nuclear Commission on Human Rights in 1946. "The Economic and Social Council, understanding that experts in human rights were not necessarily experts in the rights of women, established a Commission [on the Status of Women] which was to concern itself specially with those rights,"[28] says Bodil Begtrup.

The representatives of the Sub-Commission on the Status of Women are independent women's experts nominated on the grounds of their individual qualifications and with a view to ensuring broad geographic representation.[29] Bodil Begtrup is elected Chair of the Sub-Commission on the Status of Women. The other delegates are: Xu Yizhen (Mrs. Way Sung New), China; Minerva Bernardino, the Dominican Republic; Hansa Mehta, India; Marie-Hélène Lefaucheux, France; Angela Jurdak, Lebanon; and Fryderyka Kalinowska, Poland.

The Sub-Commission will be chaired by an experienced politician and negotiator as Bodil Begtrup is President of the Danish National Council of Women 1946–49, while also a delegate of Denmark to the United Nations. From her work in the Commission on the Status of Women, she realizes the urgent need for Denmark to grant suffrage to women in Greenland. Working tirelessly on the Declaration by backing the demands of the Commission on the Status of Women, she manages via the Danish Prime Minister Knud Kristensen to grant equal voting rights for women in Greenland the same year the Declaration will be adopted in 1948. She is involved in establishing an association called *Modrehjaelpen* [Help to Mothers] to support mothers and their children. She is also President of another association that provides clothing for infants and an influential presence in creating a Danish branch of the Save the Children Fund.

How did Bodil Begtrup find the time to chair so many organizations for women's and children's rights during the years 1946–48? It seems that she threw herself into absorptive work and responsibilities—to enhance the conditions, especially of vulnerable children—partly as a way to cope with personal loss. She had been through a divorce a few years before she was elected delegate to the United Nations and had lived through a heartrending loss in 1941 when her only daughter died from a heart defect at age ten.[30] In an interview with the United Nations' Status of Women Radio Series after her commitment to the Commission, Bodil Begtrup will say:

> A research between widows and divorced women and other lonely mothers here in Denmark has shown that they were ever so much better off when they had an education or a hob when young. They could never be completely knocked out by life.[31]

Bodil Begtrup manages to turn the hardships in her life into a political engagement—it is she who will raise the issue of equal rights of children born out of wedlock later in the Third Committee.

The Commission on the Status of Women establishes a programme for action for the United Nations "based on four essential points: equal political rights; equal civil rights, including the very important right concerning

*Figure 3.3* Sub-Commission on the Status of Women, press conference. From left: Angela Jurdak, Lebanon; Fryderyka Kalinowska, Poland; Bodil Begtrup, Denmark, Chair; Minerva Bernardino, the Dominican Republic, and Hansa Mehta, India, 14 May 1946, Hunter College, New York.

Credit: UN Photo.

marriage; equal economic rights; and equal rights of education."[32] Bodil Begtrup says later that to:

> [S]ome people the plan for equality sounded too ambitious, but the Economic and Social Council has seen it as a kind of social revolution, and for the first time in history an international study was to be undertaken on equality of men and women from the economic, social and psychological point of view.[33]

In a male-dominated organization, creating a Commission on the Status of Women is a separatist strategy to insist upon women's rights as human rights.

## From Sub-Commission to Full Commission on the Status of Women 1946–47

It is not until June 1946 that the separatist work in the United Nations is being acknowledged more widely outside the organization: "Within the United Nations Economic and Social Council, a committee of seven women have worked on guidelines for a proposal according to United Nations principles on the equality of women,"[34] explains Bodil Begtrup in an interview with a Swedish newspaper as she arrives at Bromma Airport in Stockholm on 13 June 1946. This committee has been gathered in New York since May and has now submitted the result of its work in a digested report to the Economic and Social Council. Bodil Begtrup is the committee's only Nordic representative. She leaves her account of the New York negotiations in a presentation at the Fredrika Bremer Association in Stockholm, Sweden, before returning home to Denmark.[35]

## A Controversial Report?

The Sub-Commission's first report on the status of women was written within two weeks, in meetings held in Begtrup's hotel room. "There they could proceed more quickly than in the nine public sessions during which they needed to make explanations to representatives of women's organizations and members of the press."[36] Bodil Begtrup especially admires the experience and views of Hansa Mehta, President of the All India Women's Conference.[37] She is "impressed with the Indian Women's Charter of Rights and Duties, which Mehta brought to the meeting."[38]

When the Sub-Commission presents its report to the Commission on Human rights, Bodil Begtrup:

> [T]hought ill of both the male representatives and of Eleanor Roosevelt who "does everything to kill our report and to drag our work down. The American women's policy is against equality. Dean Gilders even

fought with hands and feet against a mention of equality in the UN Charter and now seeks to make the work difficult and provoke disagreements about details. It is indecent."[39]

The American women delegates' opposition is shared by several women's organizations in the United States, who see it as a form of segregation. Claims for equality between women and men are met with the argument that it should not be sought if it leads to worse social and economic conditions for women. Demands for emancipation should not threaten the protection that housewives enjoy through the legal and social obligation of a husband to be the breadwinner for his family or risk loss of income for women who would lack occupation upon divorcing. Equality should not jeopardize the need for special legislation against hazardous work conditions for women in industry, as well as the right to shorter working days than men since daycare is a privilege unaffordable for working women who must leave their children home with siblings.

In an American newspaper article from July 1945 entitled "Why I Am Against the Equal Rights Amendment"[40] by Alice Hamilton, President of

*Figure 3.4* Bodil Begtrup shakes hands with Mr. Stanczyk, Poland, Director of United Nations Department of Social Affairs, after her election as Chair of the Commission on the Status of Women. Elsie Bowerman, Commission Secretary, 8 February 1947, Lake Success, New York.

Credit: UN Photo.

the National Consumers League, the question is raised: "Is woman's complete emancipation worth the sacrifice of protection?" Author Alice Hamilton is the first woman to be appointed to the faculty of Harvard University. At the time of publication of her article, forty-three national organizations have publicly opposed the Equal Rights Amendment, including the American Association of University Women. The opposition to the amendment appears to interpret 'equality' as being treated *as men* and therefore eroding legislation protective of women during pregnancy and rights to economic compensation after divorce.

## Subtle Barriers to Women Leadership?

The Sub-Commission on the Status of Women faces resistance toward their work in the United Nations administration as well. The translations of documents with which the Secretariat is to assist them are not being prioritized, the New York media is ridiculing their work, and the Commission on Human Rights is ignoring their demands.

On 13 May 1946, Mr. Tomlinson, Executive Officer of the Economic and Social Council, writes a telegram to Chair Bodil Begtrup in acknowledgment of the formal protest received by the Secretariat from the Sub-Commission on the Status of Women regarding inadequate services for the translation of documents from French into English. In the letters between Mr. Tomlinson and Bodil Begtrup, the Secretariat is described as reluctant to respond efficiently to the requests of the Sub-Commission, whose work is hindered when delegates are unable to read reports and drafts of the bill of rights.

Would the Sub-Commission be given greater support as a full Commission?

Bodil Begtrup proceeds to "lobby on behalf of a full Commission by speaking daily in New York at the breakfast meetings of various organizations, participating in a radio broadcast together with representatives of a number of US women's organizations."[41]

She gains influence with the Secretary-General, Trygve Lie, who is also Scandinavian, and they greet each other by their first names, which is a sign of friendship in their cultures. "Pleasant though this experience was, she felt dismayed about having to seek out like a supplicant among high-ranking men. 'This was the first time that I as a free Danish citizen felt that I belonged to an oppressed group'," she recalls.[42]

When Dorothy Kenyon and Eleanor Roosevelt openly express opposition to a full Commission, Bodil Begtrup feels betrayed by the influential women delegates from the United States.[43] In a speech to the Economic and Social Council on May 28, Bodil Begtrup responds by arguing that since the work on the legal and social status of women "covers the condition of half the population of the world," it should not be dependent on another commission. "To say, as some had in recent days, that women's problems should not be separate from those of men was 'purely unrealistic and academic'." [44]

When the Economic and Social Council addresses the report on the composition of full commissions from the Commission on Human Rights, several male delegates express skepticism about granting full status to the Commission on the Status of Women.

The United States male delegate Winant "announces that the United States delegation agrees with the recommendations made by all nuclear Commissions concerning the composition of the full Commissions, with the exception of the Temporary Social Commission and the Sub-Commission on the Status of Women."[45] Mr. Winant says that the United States instead attaches special importance to the creation of a sub-commission on freedom of information and the press. The United Kingdom male delegate Noel-Baker states, "the Government of the United Kingdom agrees with Mr. Winant's suggestion concerning the establishment of the commissions."[46] The male delegate of Peru, Arca Parró, "expresses his sympathy with the recommendations of the Sub-Commission on the Status of Women, but feels that the Sub-Commission should not be given independent status."[47]

The skeptical stance in the Commission on Human Rights toward a full Commission on the Status of Women is not shared by the Third Committee, which approves the creation of the Commission on the Status of Women without debate and sends it onward to a United Nations General Assembly plenary session, where it is approved.[48]

As the Sub-Commission turns into a full Commission, its members are now nominated by the Economic and Social Council as state representatives. Bodil Begtrup is elected Chair in the Commission on the Status of Women (followed by Marie-Hélène Lefaucheux, France, in January 1948); Jessie Street, Vice-Chair (followed by Amalia de Castillo Ledón, Mexico, in January 1948); and Eydokia Uralova, Rapporteur (followed by Alice Kandalft Cosma, Syria, in January 1948).

## Should Equal Representation Be Required by Member States?

The full Commission on the Status of Women is invited to hold their meetings parallel to the Commission on Human Rights at Lake Success in New York. It is rather tricky to find locations in the New York area that can welcome all delegates to the Economic and Social Council and the General Assembly. The General Assembly will convene in August 1946 in the New York City Building (present-day Queens Museum) in Flushing Meadows Park in Queens and continues to do so until 1948. In many ways, the building resembles the northern façade of the White House with its exterior colonnades and limestone corners. It had been built for the World's Fair in 1940, exhibiting art for 'the World of Tomorrow.' The New York City Building was beautifully located overlooking the park and with the circled flags of the fifty-one Member States waving in the wind at Flushing Meadows Park. It was a convenient location as diplomats living in the area and the city had two airports (LaGuardia Airport and Idlewild Airport, the latter of which has since been renamed JFK) that would aid the United Nations delegations flying in from all the corners of the world. (Symbolically, in 1964, the beautiful *Unisphere*, a huge steel globe, was built in front of the building on the lawn, symbolizing the theme of the following World's Fair, 'Peace through Understanding.' A smaller *Unisphere* can also be found in Islamabad, Pakistan).

The Economic and Social Council and its commissions meet in Lake Success at the Sperry Gyroscope Plant, Northern State Parkway and Lakeville Road, in a low, military-like building surrounded by fields. The commissions will spend the cold winter months of January until March in 1947 and 1948 at Lake Success. As Chair of the Commission on the Status of Women, Marie-Hélène Lefaucheux of France will write sarcastically in the United Nations Bulletin, "The barren debates which followed these [political] assertions are as fatal to strict adherence to the agenda as the regular January snowfall which isolates Lake Success and makes Chairmen of commissions nervous."[49]

Even before the Commission on the Status of Women has the chance to initiate their agenda in February 1947, Bodil Begtrup presents a resolution in the General Assembly on behalf of the Danish delegation, calling on Member States to grant equal political rights to women. The resolution consists of three demands: 1) suffrage for women in all Member States, 2) that the Secretary-General communicates that all Member States must adopt measures necessary to fulfill the purposes and ends of the Charter on suffrage for women, and 3) that the political rights of women in new Member States be considered during membership application. The two first parts of the resolution are adopted unanimously in the General Assembly. The third is rejected.

Bodil Begtrup circulates the third part of the proposal to the other members in the Commission on the Status of Women, which asks the Security Council and the General Assembly to consider the political, civil, and economic rights of women when reviewing applications for membership in the United Nations.[50] Bodil Begtrup withdraws her proposal after a discussion on the advisability of suggesting such requirements for new Member States to the United Nations when the present ones have not met that requirement.

Had the Latin American feminist line of argument been pursued to underpin the proposal in the General Assembly, this would have raised the question of equal representation within delegations. When the equal rights of women to hold positions in the United Nations had been included in Article 8 of the UN Charter, Bertha Lutz had argued that traditionally men everywhere had been sure to inscribe their rights in legal documents. Would male delegates have accepted that the respect for their political rights not be a prerequisite for membership to the United Nations? Would they have deemed delegations as representative of their peoples if a majority did not appoint a single male delegate?

The Member States who do mention women in their treaties are praised by the Commission on the Status of Women. Jessie Street affirms at the first meeting of the full Commission that she has presented a resolution of gratitude toward countries that have included the mention of women's equality in their peace treaties: Romania, Italy, Hungary, Bulgaria, and Finland.[51]

At its first meeting as a full Commission, Bodil Begtrup suggests that the Commission use the expression 'on the Status of Women' for its title (as is used today) instead of "on the Political, Civil, and Economic Rights of Women." Alice Cosma from Syria thinks that 'Status of Women' is too general and prefers the original wording, which is closer to the Spanish version '*la Comisión de la Condición Jurídica y Social de la Mujer*.'[52] The shorter title will prevail.

## Influence over the Declaration?

Questions now arise regarding influence on the work of the International Bill of Rights in terms of representation of the Commission on the Status of Women in meetings of the Commission on Human Rights.

Mr. Humphrey of Canada informs them that the Commission on Human Rights has appointed a Sub-Committee to make a draft of a bill for its next session in the summer of 1946. He thinks it "appropriate for the Commission on the Status of Women to ask that a representative be allowed to participate in the meetings of the Human Rights Commission."[53]

Mary Sutherland of the United Kingdom[54] reckons the Commission on the Status of Women lacks "a right to ask to be represented at the committee appointed by another commission."[55] She does not deem it advisable to set up another committee for a special draft of women's rights as she suspects the Commission on Human Rights will "realize that women's rights are a part of human rights."[56] Mary Sutherland agrees with Mr. Humphrey that they can *ask* to send a representative to the Commission on Human Rights. She is supported by Dorothy Kenyon of the United States in her hesitations.[57] Mary Sutherland advises that the Commission on the Status of Women should only be represented by a single member, but the proposal is defeated by ten to four votes.[58]

The Commission on the Status of Women reports on coordination with other commissions to the Economic and Social Council, requesting to be represented at the drafting committee of the Commission on Human Rights by three members: the Chair, Vice-Chair and Rapporteur. Preliminary drafts of the bill are to be made available to the members of the Commission on the Status of Women at the same time as these are made available to members of the Commission on Human Rights.

These decisions made in the Commission on the Status of Women for influence over the Declaration is nevertheless met by resistance from the Commission on Human Rights.

When the Commission on Human Rights discusses the document that will regulate how the newly established Commission on the Status of Women will report to the Commission on Human Rights, Chair Eleanor Roosevelt wants to *delete* the mention that the Commission on Human Rights has an interest in the political and social status of women.[59]

The male delegate Lebeau of Belgium agrees that 'there might be some duplication' and that the Commission on the Status of Women should report directly to the Economic and Social Council.[60]

This proposal by Belgium, if accepted by the Commission on Human Rights, will fail to request the Commission on Human Rights to explain how consideration is given to the status of women relative to articles discussed. Moreover, it risks marginalizing the work of the Commission on the Status of Women since they will lack the ability to raise points of contention if they are not responsible for reporting directly to the Commission on Human Rights on the various drafts of the bill.

Three delegates in the Commission on Human Rights resist a marginalization of the Commission on the Status of Women in the work to draft the Declaration; a Southern female delegate (Hansa Mehta, India), a Socialist male delegate (Mr. Tepliakov, the Soviet Union), and another male delegate from the former colonies (Mr. Romulo, the Philippines).[61]

When Eleanor Roosevelt presents the decision to be taken, she formulates it as merely a question of 'some duplication' in wording if the document on the work process is to mention the Commission on Human Rights' 'interest in the status of women' when there is now a full Commission on the Status of Women.[62] The proposal is met with opposition by the USSR delegate Mr. Tepliakov, who does "not want the words 'status of women' to be deleted" and argues that in relation to an International Bill of Rights, "the Commission on Human Rights is entitled to deal with all questions within the field of human rights."[63]

Hansa Mehta of India agrees with Mr. Tepliakov—"when discussing the Bill of Rights, the status of women will have to be considered in co-operation with the Commission on the Status of Women," she says.[64] Mr. Romulo of the Philippines stands behind Hansa Mehta by confirming that the status of women is "an integral part of whatever Bill of Rights will be discussed."[65]

Eleanor Roosevelt revises the initial proposal in light of the opposition from Hansa Mehta, Mr. Tepliakov, and Mr. Romulo. The Belgian suggestion that the Commission on the Status of Women will have to communicate with the Economic and Social Council instead of directly with the Commission on Human Rights is not followed.

Eleanor Roosevelt sums up the opinions expressed: that the Commission on Human Rights will have to develop a base for cooperation with the Commission on the Status of Women but adds the resolution "lest they [the Commission on Human Rights] find themselves at odds with that Commission's recommendation."[66]

If Eleanor Roosevelt thinks that this will prevent influence by the Commission on the Status of Women, if and when they disagree with proposals on different parts of the Declaration, she is misled in her assumptions. The Commission on the Status of Women will push not only to report directly to the Commission on Human Rights but, even more importantly, to have at least two representatives present at all meetings in which the Declaration is being discussed. Even though they have no voting rights on the different proposals by delegates in the Commission on Human Rights, their presence will be noticeable throughout the drafting process.

Eleanor Roosevelt's friend and colleague Katherine Pollack Ellickson writes in a speech on 4 February 1942, a few years before the creation of the United Nations:

> We assumed that the battle for women's rights had been won. We were the equals of men intellectually and, like the graduates of Harvard or Berkley, we would make our way in the world. We would have a profession and continue it, even if we married. Our views were colored by those of the older generation of feminists on the college faculty who had battled against great odds and won. They had made good—why shouldn't we? We overlooked the fact that they were all single. They had succeeded in following in men's footsteps, but they had not tackled the problem of combining children and professional activity.[67]

Katherine Pollack Ellickson will work with Eleanor Roosevelt during her years as Executive Director of the American President's Commission on the Status of Women in the sixties. Thus, Eleanor Roosevelt's initial opposition to a Commission on the Status of Women changes with age and may be owe in part to the inspiration of witnessing the change that the Commission on the Status of Women will be able to pursue in the United Nations.

## Notes

1. Third Committee, summary record 98th meeting, October 9, 1948, A/C.3/SR.98, 108.
2. "Plan för samarbete kan rensa upp i världens slum" [Plan for Cooperation Can Clean Up in the World's Slum], *Dagens Nyheter*, from the Social Council at Lake Success, January 22, 1947.
3. Ibid.
4. Ibid.
5. Ibid.
6. *Open Letter to the Women of the World*, United Nations, First session of the General Assembly, 1946.
7. United Nations, General Assembly, verbatim record 7th meeting, 14 January 1946, A.PV.7, 102.
8. Ibid., 105.
9. Ibid., 105.
10. "Sverige deltar i flera grenar av FN:s arbete" [Sweden Participates in Several of the UN Branches's Work] by Per Persson, *Svenska Dagbladet*, New York, April 30, 1946.

11. "FN gick emot flyktingjakt" [The UN Objected to Hunt on Refugees], *Svenska Dagbladet*, New York (TT fr. Reuter), June 23, 1946.
12. "FN:s tjugostatskommission" [The Twenty-States-Commission of the UN] by S. Å, *Dagens Nyheters*, New York, July 15, 1946.
13. Street, *Truth or Repose*, 96.
14. Ibid., 98.
15. Ibid., 127.
16. "Sverige deltar i flera grenar av FN:s arbete" [Sweden Participates in Several of the UN Branches's Work] by Per Persson, *Svenska Dagbladet*, New York, April 30, 1946.
17. "Mänskligheten och paragrafer" [Humanity and Paragraphs] by Agda Rössel, *Svenska Dagbladet*, September 14, 1956.
18. Ibid.
19. Ibid.
20. *Human Rights—Comments and Interpretations*. A Symposium, ed. UNESCO. Introduction by Jacques Maritain, Paris, July 25, 1948, 1.
21. *Human Rights—Comments and Interpretations*. A Symposium, ed. by UNESCO. Introduction by Jacques Maritain, Paris, July 25, 1948.
22. *Human Rights—Comments and Interpretations*, 1.
23. Mahatma Ghandi, "A Letter Addressed to the Director-General of UNESCO," Ghangi Colony, New Delhi, May 25, 1947, in *Human Rights—Comments and Interpretations*. A Symposium, ed. by UNESCO. Introduction by Jacques Maritain, Paris, July 25, 1948, 3.
24. *Human Rights—Comments and Interpretations*. A Symposium, ed. by UNESCO. Introduction by Jacques Maritain, Paris, July 25, 1948.
25. Commission on Human Rights, summary record 26th meeting, held in closed session, December 3, 1947, Geneva, E/CN.4/SR.26, 17.
26. Bernardino, *Lucha, Agonía y Esperanza*, 115–18 (trans. from Spanish to English by author).
27. Doris H. Linder, "Equality for Women: The Contribution of Scandinavian Women at the United Nations, 1946–66," *Scandinavian Studies* 73, no. 2 (2001): 174.
28. General Assembly, verbatim record 182d plenary meeting, December 10, 1948, A/PV.182, 891–93.
29. Kristine Midtgaard, "Bodil Begtrup and the Universal Declaration of Human Rights: Individual Agency, Transnationalism and Intergovernmentalism in Early UN Human Rights," *Scandinavian Journal of History* 36, no. 4 (2011): 484.
30. Kristine Kjærsgaard, "Love and Emotions in the Diplomatic World: The Relationship between Bodil Begtrup's Public and Private Lives, 1937–1956," in *Biography, Gender and History: Nordic Perspectives*, ed. Erla Hulda Halldórsdóttir et al. (Turku, Finland: kulttuurhistoria, University of Turku, 2016), 128.
31. United Nations, "Interview with Bodil Begtrup," in *UN Status of Women Radio Series*. Transcripts of interviews, written by the United Nations, January 1949, 1.
32. General Assembly, verbatim record 182d plenary meeting, December 10, 1948, A/PV.182, 891–93.
33. Ibid.
34. "Kvinnoförslag i FN om likställigheten" [Women's Proposal in the United Nations on Equality], *Dagens Nyheter*, June 13, 1946.
35. Ibid.
36. Linder, "Equality for Women," 174.
37. Ibid.
38. Ibid.
39. Midtgaard, "Bodil Begtrup and the Universal Declaration of Human Rights," 485.

40. Alice Hamilton, "Why I Am Against the Equal Rights Amendment," *Ladies' Home Journal* (July 1945).
41. Linder, "Equality for Women," 175.
42. Ibid.
43. Ibid., 176.
44. Ibid., 176.
45. Economic and Social Council, summary record 5th meeting, May 31, 1946, E/SR.19, 36.
46. Ibid., 38.
47. Ibid., 40.
48. Linder, "Equality for Women," 176.
49. Marie-Hélène Lefaucheux, Chair of the Commission on the Status of Women, "Work for Women's Equality of Status", *United Nations Bulletin* (1948): 343.
50. Commission on the Status of Women, summary record of the 9th meeting, New York, February 14, 1947, E/CN.6/SR.9, 4.
51. Ibid., 7–8.
52. Ibid., 4.
53. Commission on the Status of Women, summary record 12th meeting, February 18, 1947, E/CN.6/SR.12, 7–8.
54. British Politician, Chief Woman Officer Labour Party (ed.), "The Labour Woman," Member of Ministry of Labour Women's Consultative Committee.
55. Commission on the Status of Women, summary record 12th meeting, February 18, 1947, E/CN.6/SR.12, 8.
56. Ibid.
57. Ibid.
58. Ibid., 10.
59. Commission on Human Rights, summary record 1st meeting, January 27, 1947, E/CN.4/SR.1, 6.
60. Ibid.
61. Ibid.
62. Ibid.
63. Ibid.
64. Ibid.
65. Ibid.
66. Ibid., 7.
67. "Short-Time Work for Women," by Katherine P. Ellickson, *Franklin Roosevelt Library*, February 4, 1942.

# 4 The Commission on Human Rights

## Or the 'Rights of Man'?

> But when the call to fight for freedom came, it was wonderful to see how women rose to the occasion. I vividly remember women clad in their saffron uniform marching towards Freedom.[1]
>
> —Hansa Mehta, India

### Decolonization Changes the Game

The dynamic in the United Nations changes radically during the years 1946–48 when the Universal Declaration of Human Rights is being drafted, debated, and voted through different bodies in the United Nations. At the outset, the United States and France place a strong emphasis on earlier notions of the 'Rights of Man' articulated in their respective constitutions.

When the first Committee of the General Assembly met in December 1946—before the Commission on Human Rights had initiated its work in February 1947—Mr. Pezet of France:

> [P]oints out that France has just adopted a new constitution which is preceded by a preamble confirming, renewing and modernizing the Declaration of the Rights of Man and of the Citizen. The Assembly which has adopted that constitution comprises not only citizens of metropolitan France but also the citizens of the French Union. Thus, a Declaration of the Rights of Man amplified to the scale of continents has been proclaimed.[2]

A new constitution has been accepted in Oct 1946, leading to the French Fourth Republic, but, contrary to the claim of Mr. Pezet, its accomplishments from 1946 to 1958 will lead to the economic development of the French state, not necessarily to increased rights of the people living under its colonial rule. As former colonies of the United Kingdom and France gain their independence in the postwar years, new Member States to the United Nations send their delegations to participate—challenging dominant narratives.

The first time the wording 'human rights' is used in a document in the United Nations is in its Charter to be listed and defined through the Declaration of Human Rights. As delegates from divergent contexts meet in New York to discuss the origins of the 'Rights of Man,' it will become obvious that the historical trajectory of Western imperialism would be met with opposition in the debates.

India had already been a member of the United Nations by 1945 and had voted for the Charter that same year, but, while gaining full independence in 1947, India sends a delegate to the Commission on Human Rights famous for having presented the 'National Flag' that same year on behalf of the women of India—Hansa Mehta.

*Figure 4.1* Hansa Mehta, India, and Chair Eleanor Roosevelt, the United States, the Commission on Human Rights, 1 June 1949, Lake Success, New York. They were working on an International Convention on Human Rights.

Credit: UN Photo/Marvin Bolotsky.

As India is represented by a female politician and human rights activist in the Commission on Human Rights, politically sensitive questions will arise in the Commission. How far, in terms of colonial territories, will the concept of human rights reach? Will France, the United Kingdom, and other colonial powers in the United Nations involve *all* people under their rule in any capacity during the process of drafting a *Universal* Declaration of Human Rights? The initial view of the Western Member States seemed to have been that 'human rights' were equivalent to the 'Rights of Man,' which had historically been referring to male White citizens.

When the Commission on Human Rights meets in 1947 at Lake Success, New York, Jim Crow laws remain in place in the Southern states of America. This is a politically controversial issue that the Soviet delegates, especially Mr. Bogomolov, will avail himself of whenever possible as a rebuttal to critiques regarding the lack of political and civil liberties in the Socialist Soviet Union. At one point, Eleanor Roosevelt refutes Mr. Bogomolov by saying that she will welcome Soviet inspection of American hospitals, schools, and factories if the Soviet delegation will allow an American delegation the same insight.

These were just some of the political tensions that would be felt by delegates in the Commission on Human Rights as the work on the Declaration densified underlying disagreements and unsettled power relations.

## Hansa Mehta—a Freedom Fighter

At the first session of the full Commission on Human Rights on 27 January in 1947 at Lake Success in New York, Hansa Mehta is the delegate who proposes Eleanor Roosevelt as Chair, "paying tribute to her work as Chair of the Nuclear Commission on Human Rights."[3] Mr. Romulo of the Philippines moves that nominations be closed directly after Hansa Mehta nominates Eleanor Roosevelt. The United States is at this instance the only so-called 'Great Power' represented by a woman. Eleanor Roosevelt is unanimously elected Chair. Mr. Romulo is one of few besides Hansa Mehta in the Commission on Human Rights who represents a newly independent Member State.

At this constituent meeting of the Commission on Human Rights, Mr. Dukes of the United Kingdom nominates Mr. Chang of China as Vice-Chairman—a wise election since Mr. Chang, as a professor of philosophy and former diplomat, is sensitively attentive to the moral differences and perspectives of the delegates in the Commission. In his capacity as China's representative in Turkey (from 1942 to 1945) right before his appointment to the United Nations, Mr. Chang has pointed to parallels between the values of Confucianism and Islam in his diplomatic dealings. He is of the belief that Western thinkers such as Voltaire built on Chinese philosophies on the notion of rights. Mr. Chang is unanimously elected by the delegates in the Commission on Human Rights as Vice-Chair.

Mr. Romulo nominates another delegate from a newly independent state, Mr. Malik, delegate of Lebanon, as Rapporteur. Mr. Malik will later serve as Chair in the Third Committee. Mr. Malik is a philosopher who has grown up within both Christian and Islamic traditions. As such, right at the start of establishing the order in the Commission on Human Rights, the smaller states and the only two female representatives have voice and influence.

At the second meeting of the Commission on Human Rights, Hansa Mehta raises her first critique of the prevailing dominant discourse of Member States, recalling that:

> [T]he Government of South Africa has maintained the position . . . that there has been no violation of human rights in South Africa since there exists no written definition of human rights as such within the framework of the United Nations. The Government of the United Kingdom has taken a similar attitude by suggesting that the dispute between India and South Africa might be referred to the International Court of Justice.[4]

Hansa Mehta "considers it the justification of the Commission that pleas of this nature should not be allowed to be advanced within the forum of the United Nations in the future."[5] Her hope is that if the Declaration is drafted as "a simple and forthright document" and with the "assurance that there will be adequate machinery for its enforcement" then the current work of the Commission on Human Rights is to create a safeguard through a Convention to which people can refer "whenever human rights are violated in States Members of the United Nations."[6]

Hansa Mehta will serve not only as delegate to the Commission of Human Rights but also on the Sub-Commission on the Status of Women and to the United Nations Educational, Scientific, and Cultural Organization. As a representative of India, she actively campaigns for the inclusion of equal rights for women within the United Nations.

Hansa Mehta has previously been a member of the Bombay Legislative Council and the Constituent Assembly of India and served as Parliamentary Secretary to the Minister of Education and Health. She has graduated with honors from Baroda College where her father was a professor of philosophy. In her book *Indian Woman*, she recalls that even though she was admitted to Baroda College, there had been no real space prepared for the female students, who were given only a tiny room by the stairs:

> [V]ery few women went in for University education. We were about half a dozen in the Baroda College. My sister, myself and another girl were the only women students in a class of one hundred and fifty. Though there was no bar against admission of women to higher education, it seemed that women who were admitted were more or less on sufferance.[7]

Hansa Mehta disregarded the strictures of caste to marry for love. Her marriage to Dr. Jivraj Mehta from the Vaishya community results in her excommunication from her community, even though her family approves of the marriage. She muses over the controversy in *Indian Woman*: "It was most amusing that they did not excommunicate the entire family which was usually done, but only me, who was willingly going out of the caste!"[8]

Hansa Mehta later studies journalism and sociology in the United Kingdom where she meets Sarojini Naidu and Rajkumari Amrit Kaur, who inspire her to join the struggle for Indian freedom. She is jailed twice for her active involvement in 1930 and 1932—as are so many other women as they picket shops selling foreign goods. The non-violent strategy of boycotting campaigns against economic exploitation by the United Kingdom are initially not unlawful; women join by the thousand, inspired by the call by Mahatma Gandhi. Even when later declared illegal, women continue to join the struggle, risking their individual freedom to free India. Hansa Mehta sees Gandhi's call as the inspiration that brought women out of their homes, the beginning of what became a political awakening in which women risked their personal safety. She recalls this historical moment years later while writing her book: "It thrills me even today to think of the first batch of Desh Sevikas I led to the field jointly with Shrimati Jayaben Kanuga. It was 1 May 1930, when we sallied forth in hundreds to picket the Bhuleshwar shops."[9]

## 'Men' Will Not Mean 'Women'

When the Commission on Human Rights meets in 1947 to consider drafts to the Declaration from the Nuclear Commission in New York, the formulations used are taken under critical scrutiny. Eleanor Roosevelt has not reacted to the use of 'all men' in the initial to Article 1 by male representatives of France, Australia, and the United Kingdom, which is now brought to debate by Hansa Mehta. The suggestions submitted by the representative of France to Article 1 reads:

> *All men* are *brothers* being endowed with reason, members of one family. They are free and possess equal dignity and rights.[10]
>
> [author's emphasis]

Hansa Mehta, the only female delegate in the Commission on Human Rights besides Eleanor Roosevelt, objects to the use of 'all men' in Article 1, arguing that Member States can use this to restrict women's rights rather than expand them since women are not necessarily regarded as included by that wording.

Would stating that 'all *men* have the right to vote' in the Declaration be interpreted as including the rights of women in all Member States? Hansa Mehta has good reason to challenge Eleanor Roosevelt on this point.

Women have been vital for the Indian independence movement through all-women demonstrations—the *Satyagraha* movement and boycotts of British merchandise—and the *Swadeshi* movement. The boycott strategy was so decisive since the colonial exploitation to 'connect markets' was built apart from obvious military power by means of business legislation and monetary management. These discriminatory business legislations were in place during the independence movement, and it was critical to combat the oppressive violence through non-violent means, and the economic exploitation through boycotting means, as the administration of trade was still in the hands of the colonizers. Indian nationalists, including Gandhi, see it as women's duty to support the independence movement. Even so, women's equal right to vote is a struggle women have to fight for themselves.

Since 1920, there had been limited suffrage for women under colonial rule: In certain states of India, women had the ability to vote if they were married, owned property, and were educated, which in reality meant that not many women were actually granted this right. In 1930, while the United Kingdom had dominated the administration of the educational system in India, only two percent of women were literate. Hansa Mehta saw this as one of the main obstacles toward the realization of women's political rights.

In 1910, an Indian woman named Sarala Devi Chaudhurani (1872–1945) founded the organization the Great Group of Indian Women, which was devoted to women's right to education. Sarala Devi Chaudhurani was a feminist and a nationalist—active in both the social reformist movement and the independence movement—and realized the need for creating women-only organizations in India. Amongst the first was the Women's India Association (WIA), founded in 1917 to represent all women regardless of class, caste, or ethnicity, although members were mostly from the higher classes. The National Council of Women in India (NCWI), founded in 1925, directed their engagement toward the government, offering counseling and advice regarding women's rights, an even more elitist organization in terms of members. These separatist formations sprung from the realization that discussions with the colonial administration would lead nowhere and that only supporting the nationalist movement would not automatically lead to suffrage for women.

The All India Women's Conference (AIWC), founded in 1927, was the organization that succeeded best in representing the diversity of Indian women. As illiteracy amongst women in India was as high as 98 percent in the thirties during colonial rule, the conference was initially called the All India Women's Educational Conference. Hansa Mehta joins the conference early on and recalls, "It was realized that the educational backwardness of Indian women was due to social evils like child marriages, purdah etc. which hampered their progress. Unless these evils were removed, there was no hope for their advancement."[11] The All India Women's Conference heralds the campaign to pass the "Hindu Child Marriage Bill" called the

*Sarada Act* that connects women's right to education with the question of child marriage. The women of the conference contend that child marriages are a hindrance to women's emancipation and to their right to education. The question of child marriage is one of the few issues that unite the whole women's movement. The government responds to the *Sarada Act* by stating that the proposal should not include Muslim women since the Muslim society is against the Act.

Muslim women in the All India Women's Conference write a petition to the government:

> We, speaking also on behalf of the Muslim women of India, assert that it is only a small section of Mussalman men who have been approaching your excellency and demanding exemption from the Sarada Act. This Act affects girls and women far more than it affects men and we deny their right to speak on our behalf.[12]

Hansa Mehta, however, is not satisfied with the bill, which is far from the resolution against child marriage that she initially proposed during the All India Women's Conference. "The bill as it was ultimately accepted was very much watered down. As a result, the Sarada Act was never effective in the prevention of child marriage."[13]

In 1945–46, Hansa Mehta is President of the All India Women's Conference—the same year she serves in the Sub-Commission on the Status of Women. As President of the All India Women's Conference in 1945, she proposes a Declaration of Women's Rights.

When the Constituent Assembly of India meets on 9 December 1946, fifteen of its members are women, and a number of them, including Sarojini Naidu, Durgabai Deshmukh, Renuka Ray, and Hansa Mehta, are elected to the Draft committee to frame the Constitution for India.[14] In the Draft committee, Hansa Mehta expresses that the Hindu Personal Law applied under the colonial period is dividing the country and that a uniform civil code is required. This Uniform Civil Code must, in her view, be in advance of the most progressive of the personal laws in the country.

In Parliament, Hansa Mehta and her female colleague had proposed a separation of the Hindu Code Bill into two—one dealing with the right to divorce and the other dealing with women's right to inherit family property. This was a strategic response to the divided opposition against these two parts of women's rights. The only way to get both rights passed in Parliament was to divide the larger bill into two separate ones. Their aim was total enfranchisement and economic independence for women in India. Hansa Mehta writes in *Indian Woman* that she wants women in India to be regarded by the state as individuals, not having their rights dependent on a husband or the family.

The interdependence of political rights and socioeconomic rights is felt through the experiences of women like Hansa Mehta, who has witnessed how women's right to vote is dependent on their reproductive and sexual rights that are in turn connected to equal rights regarding marriage and a woman's economic independence. When the Universal Declaration of Human Rights is debated in the United Nations, for Hansa Mehta human rights are not empty words but lived realities responding to the needs of women.

## Philosophical Debate or Legal Enforcement of Equality?

Mr. Dukes, delegate of the United Kingdom, relates the general discussion on drafting "the International Bill of Human Rights" back to the 'civilizing mission' of his country by stating that "The United Kingdom has always been in the forefront of the fight for human rights."[15] He argues that "the British Government has always, everywhere, fostered the emancipation of the human person, along with the promotion of education and of social and economic progress."[16] Hansa Mehta asks in response to this statement in the Commission on Human Rights that "the general debate be brought to an end so that the Commission can consider the draft" she has submitted, which includes the notion of equality and non-discrimination.[17]

The male delegates in the Commission on Human Rights, conversely, seem eager to continue their discussion of the underlying philosophical principles of the 'Rights of Man.' They want to discuss the very foundation of human rights and ponder long-windedly on the question of whether 'Man' has rights because endowed with reason or not, which would separate 'men' from animals. They argue passionately religious and secular views regarding whether human beings are born with dignity and if the concept of dignity has to be related to Creationism. Should reference to God or Nature even exist in the Declaration? The Soviet delegation thinks not, and as the Declaration will have to be adopted by governments with divergent ideological systems—both religious and secular—an agreement will have to be reached on conflicting ideological grounds.

Mr. Malik seems to enjoy the more philosophical debates rather than legalistic formalities and adds to the discussion in the Commission that when working out a Declaration on human rights: "it is not politicians and diplomats alone who were concerned with this question; the advice of poets, prophets and philosophers should be asked."[18]

Hansa Mehta, however, wants the discussions in the Commission on Human Rights to focus on actual resolutions from different countries instead of general philosophical debates. She asks, again, at the second meeting, "for a discussion on the resolution which she submitted, in order to bring the debate back to specific points."[19] Uruguay and the United Kingdom agree that the Indian draft should be studied. Mr. Malik then suggests that "the Commission should consider the Indian draft resolution as the basis of discussion."[20] It is decided that a drafting group should study various drafts to the Declaration. What is of prominence in the draft resolution proposed by the Indian delegation is that it deals with equality.[21] The second paragraph in the Indian proposal states that "Every *human being* has the right to *equality*, without distinction of race, *sex*, language, religion, nationality or political belief."[22]

## A Legally Binding Bill or an Educative Declaration?

It was initially not clear whether the Commission would be assigned the task of drafting a legally binding bill, a declaration, or both. When Eleanor Roosevelt presumes that "everyone seems in favor of a general Bill or Declaration" and not a legally binding document, she is interrupted by Hansa Mehta, who does not think that a "mere Declaration will be sufficient."[23] Informed by her experience in the First Constituent Assembly of India, Hansa Mehta yearns to see legal provisions for implementing universal human rights put in place.

It is decided in the Commission on Human Rights that a legally binding bill will be drawn up and submitted together with the Declaration to the Economic and Social Council.[24]

The Commission on Human Rights will now devote a whole day to studying means of implementing human rights.[25] Eleanor Roosevelt lets Hansa Mehta introduce the discussions on the means of implementation.[26]

Hansa Mehta "points out that the form of the Bill of Human Rights is of great importance to her government."[27] She uses irony in her argumentation referring back to the earlier discussion in the Commission: "It can either be in the nature of a vague resolution, including mystic and psychological principles, or it can be an instrument binding on all the Member States."[28] Hansa Mehta says she is "in favor of the latter form as it will be in accordance with the Charter" and she feels it essential that the Bill has an "imperative character."[29]

After this statement by India, Australian representative Mr. Hodgson proposes the creation of an "International Court of Human Rights."[30] Mr. Hodgson says that "this Court will be the Central Appeal Court to which States, groups of individuals, and even single individuals can appeal when all domestic possibilities of appeal have been exhausted."[31] Mr. Romulo is the first to respond to this suggestion and says that he is entirely in agreement with the proposal for the creation of an "International Court of Human Rights" and that "the government of the Philippine Republic is prepared to include all the provisions of the Bill in its Constitution."[32] He sees the rights and freedoms as a safeguard against tyranny and a way to free people under colonial rule.

Other delegates are not as optimistic toward a creation of an "International Court of Human Rights." The male representatives of Chile, the Soviet Union, Belgium, and the United Kingdom want to wait to discuss a court and implementation system for the rights set forth in the Declaration until such a document has been passed by the General Assembly.

Eleanor Roosevelt agrees that the question of implementation must wait, as the United States government feels it needs to be sure it can accept all rights listed in the final document.

Hansa Mehta seems rather irritated by the procrastinations and "wonders whether the Commission should be satisfied with an academic discussion of a Bill of Rights or whether it wishes to implement such a Bill."[33] Hansa Mehta questions the weight of the work being done in the Commission on Human Rights, postulating that "agreement must be reached on the principle upon which the Bill will be applied, otherwise the existence of the Commission can not be justified."[34] She is seconded by Toni Sender, representative of the American Federation of Labor, who adds that:

> [T]he peoples must have faith in the United Nations and consequently, if it is decided to draft an International Bill of Rights, it must be shown that it is not merely a matter of empty words, but that decisions made will be applied and enforced.[35]

Representing an organization with consultative status, Toni Sender can participate in the debates but does not vote on any parts in the Declaration. As she is active in the debates of the Commission, Mr. Humphrey says she "interpreted her consultative function rather widely."[36]

The critique raised by both Hansa Mehta and Toni Sender—that if the Commission is to draft a legally binding bill on human rights this calls for a discussion on the means of implementing such a bill, otherwise these are mere empty words. Mr. Dukes says he fears that he has "given the impression" that his government "is not anxious to apply the Bill of Human Rights." He therefore wishes to "make it quite clear that this is not so. It is simply a matter of avoiding commitments which governments will later hesitate to accept."[37]

It remains undetermined at this juncture whether Member States are to vote separately for a Declaration and a Bill later in the General Assembly. Hansa Mehta hopes that the Declaration will lead to a legally binding document and feels that the draft resolution "should be used by the Commission as a basis to discuss the form, contents, application, and implementation of an International Bill of Rights."[38] When the Commission on Human Rights reports to the Economic and Social Council in March 1947, Hansa Mehta suggests a general Act stating that the General Assembly has the primary responsibility for upholding the respect for human rights.[39]

## Notes

1. Hansa Mehta, *Indian Woman* (Delhi, Baroda: Butala & Company, 1981), 65.
2. William Schabas, *The Universal Declaration of Human Rights: I Volume The Travaux Préparatoires* (London: Oxford University Press, 2013), 88.
3. Commission on Human Rights, summary record 1st meeting, January 27, 1947, E/CN.4/SR.1, 4.

4. Commission on Human Rights, summary record 2nd meeting, January 27, 1947, E/CN.4/SR.2, 3.
5. Ibid.
6. Ibid.
7. Mehta, *Indian Woman*, 64.
8. Ibid., 62.
9. Ibid., 66.
10. Commission on Human Rights, Drafting Committee. "Revised Suggestions Submitted by the Representative of France for Articles of the International Declaration of Rights," June 20, 1947, E/CN.4/AC.1/W.2/Rev.2, p.1.
11. Mehta, "Introduction," in *Indian Woman*.
12. Forbes, Geraldine, *Women in Modern India* (New York: Cambridge University Press, 1996), 89.
13. Mehta, "Introduction," in *Indian Woman*, ix.
14. Letha Kumari, *Women in Politics: Participation and Governance* (Delhi: Authorspress, 2006), 10.
15. Commission on Human Rights, summary record 8th meeting, January 31, 1947, E/CN.4/SR.8, 2.
16. Ibid.
17. Ibid., 3.
18. Commission on Human Rights, summary record 9th meeting, February 1, 1947, E/CN.4/SR.9, 3.
19. Ibid., 6.
20. Commission on Human Rights, summary record 10th meeting, February 1, 1947, E/CN.4/SR.10, 2.
21. Commission on Human Rights, summary record 13th meeting, February 4, 1947, E/CN.4/SR.13, 5.
22. Draft of a Resolution for the General Assembly Submitted by the Representative of India, January 31, 1947, E/CN.4/11, 1.
23. Commission on Human Rights, summary record 14th meeting, February 4, 1947, E/CN.4/SR.14, 7.
24. Ibid.
25. Ibid.
26. Commission on Human Rights, summary record 15th meeting, February 5, 1947, E/CN.4/SR.15, 2.
27. Ibid.
28. Ibid.
29. Ibid.
30. Ibid.
31. Ibid., 3.
32. Ibid., 3.
33. Ibid., 5.
34. Ibid., 5.
35. Ibid., 6.
36. John P. Humphrey, *Human Rights & the United Nations: A Great Adventure* (Dobbs Ferry, NY: Transnational Publishers, 1984), 25.
37. Commission on Human Rights, summary record 15th meeting, February 5, 1947, E/CN.4/SR.15, 6–7.
38. Commission on Human Rights, summary record 10th meeting, February 1, 1947, E/CN.4/SR.10, 1–2.
39. Economic and Social Council, summary record 68th meeting, Friday March 14, 1947, E/439, 103.

# 5 The Commission on the Status of Women

## On Sisterhood

> Do the countries of the world realize that they have immense source of wealth lying at their thresholds unused. What is this wealth? It is womanhood.[1]
>
> —Begum Hamid Ali, India.

The Commission on the Status of Women does not result from a Western push for gender equality within the United Nations—the first full Commission consists of a majority of women delegates from Southern Member States. The Commission on the Status of Women becomes a way for women to join efforts across ideological lines between Member States. Women delegates are a minority in their own countries' delegations, within which their interests can easily be silenced by conflicting national agendas that superseded them. By forming a Commission, women make their demands more difficult to ignore. Delegations—when confronted by a whole Commission—cannot easily dismiss women's rights as mere individual complaints that concern only a few states. The Commission on the Status of Women addresses all Member States, and women's rights are pushed as a universal concern beyond the Northern/Southern and Western/Eastern divides. On the other hand, there also exist divisions within the Commission: The American women delegates question several of the joint demands, but as they are in the minority—even though representatives of one of the largest delegations—their influence within the Commission on the Status of Women in its initial years of 1946–48 is limited.

During the winter of 1947–48, the Commission on the Status of Women holds their meetings at Lake Success in New York, traveling back and forth to Manhattan where most of the women delegates are accommodated. Several of the delegates have come from afar to be able to join the meetings in the United Nations; when the Commission on the Status of Women meets in January 1948 in New York, there is a whole floor of the Empire State Building on Thirty-Fourth Street and Fifth Avenue, reserved for the women delegates during their stay.[2] Mary Sutherland, traveling from the United Kingdom, stays on the sixty-first floor of the Empire State Building. Amalia de Castillo Ledón, traveling from Mexico, stays at 6206 Empire State

Building. Jessie Street, who travels all the way from Australia, stays at 4510 Empire State Building, and Begum Hamid Ali, traveling from India, stays at 6212 Empire State Building.[3] It must have been a rather stark contrast between staying in Times Square in bustling Manhattan and convening outside the city in the Sperry Plant, with its plain landscape.

From day one, the Commission on the Status of Women has had an agenda: to place women's rights at the forefront in the conversation process of forming the Declaration. Of special concern to the Commission on the Status of Women are the following changes they would like made in the Declaration: 1) The preamble should mention "equality of women and men," as in the preamble of the Charter; 2) Article 1 must have a more inclusive wording than 'all men' and 'like brothers'; 3) Article 2 must include "sex" in the non-discrimination list, as in the Charter; 4) Article 16 on marriage is to mention a) the right to divorce, b) the social security of married and divorced women, c) a formulation prohibiting child marriage, and d) a statement regarding the principle of monogamy; and finally 5) Article 21 on suffrage is to repeat "equality of men and women."

By formulating a joint strategy, the Commission builds a sisterhood for change in all three instances (the Commission on Human Rights, the Third Committee, and the General Assembly) the Declaration is debated and voted through. These changes are strategically pushed by the members of the Commission on the Status of Women who are also delegates to the Commission on Human Rights (Hansa Mehta), the Third Committee (Bodil Begtrup, Minerva Bernardino, Fryderyka Kalinowska, Zuloaga, and Lakshmi Menon), and the General Assembly (Bodil Begtrup, Minerva Bernardino, and Lakshmi Menon,).

The women delegates to the full Commission on the Status of Women are appointed by their governments, so every one of them has an impressive background and expertise on women's rights. Their public appearances contrast one another in different ways. Minerva Bernardino can be found in endless official images, with her many dramatic hats and elegant suits, shaking hands with powerful people who celebrate her prominence in championing women's rights internationally. Hansa Mehta, on the other hand, can be found in fewer images, wearing her sari and sandals in the United Nations meetings.

Eleanor Roosevelt was an outspoken first lady, and her achievements have been well documented by historians. Lakshmi Menon, by contrast, has not been celebrated in historical accounts, although she seemed to have been as forceful in her words and in her deeds. In the United Nations meeting records, she is one of the women delegates who is most active in the Third Committee debates, as well as in the Commission on the Status of Women. In the United Nations photos, however, she seemed to have shied away from being photographed and is nowhere to be seen. Her words were well chosen and what she seemed to have wanted to be remembered for. Fryderyka Kalinowska is another woman delegate whose contributions in debates in

*Figure 5.1* Second session of the Commission on the Status of Women. From left: Minerva Bernardino, the Dominican Republic (representing Inter-American Commission of Women); Bodil Begtrup, Denmark; Alice Kandalft Cosma, Syria; Amalia de Castillo Ledón, Mexico; and Dorothy Kenyon, the United States, 5 January 1948, Lake Success, New York.

Credit: UN Photo.

the Third Committee is well documented yet whose achievements and public appearances are sparsely recorded elsewhere.

In the United Nations archives, twenty-one women's names are listed in different documents as delegates to the Commission on the Status of Women. Seven of them had comprised the Sub-Commission on the Status of Women.[4]

## Southern Countries in the Majority

The representatives to India in the Commission on the Status of Women will be pivotal for the feminist drive in the postwar years in the United Nations. As all three women delegates (Begum Hamid Ali, Hansa Mehta, and Lakshmi Menon) are Indian freedom fighters, they have already risked far more than mere verbal opposition—as in the United Nations sessions—for human rights and democracy.

Begum Hamid Ali organized the All India Women's Conference in the 1920s, was the chair of the Conference in 1928, as well as the President of the Sind Women's Conference in 1926. She has championed women's right to education and Muslim women's right to divorce in India.

Lakshmi Menon is a politician, and she has been Acting President for several years at the All India Women's Conference. She will oppose the oversights by colonial powers in the United Nations that explicitly state that human rights are inclusive of people living in Non-Self-Governing Territories. Lakshmi Menon later becomes Minister of State in India.

The Latin American delegates are a majority in the Commission on the Status of Women, with six delegates: Chile (Amanda Labarca); Costa Rica (Graciela Morales F. de Echeverria); the Dominican Republic (Minerva Bernardino); Guatemala (Sara Basterrechea Ramirez); Mexico (Amalia de Castillo Ledón); and Venezuela (Isabel Sánchez de Urdaneta). Three of these women were in the feminist alliance at the San Francisco Conference: Minerva Bernardino, Amalia de Castillo Ledón, and Isabel Sánchez de Urdaneta. Alongside Minerva Bernardino, the delegate who will make her voice heard, especially in the Commission on Human Rights, is Amalia de Castillo Ledón, Vice-Chair of the Commission on the Status of Women. She is Minister and President of the Court of Justice of the Nation in Mexico, the first female member of a Mexican Presidential cabinet, founder and Chair of *Club International de Mujeres*, and representative of Mexico to the Inter-American Commission of Women. In the Commission on the Status of Women, Amalia de Castillo Ledón continues the struggle for the equal recognition of women in the drafting of the Declaration, with a special focus on non-discrimination based on sex and on equal pay for women.

The Latin American women activists were relatively stronger in the postwar years than the weakened European sisters, but they faced internal obstacles as several Latin American states were ridden by anti-democratic forces, supported by external economic interests. Amanda Labarca, the founder of the National Committee for Women's Rights in 1933 and President of the Chilean Federation of Feminist Institutions in 1944, warns against anti-democratic tendencies in Chile in her book *Feminismo contemporáneo* (1947). She points to the low democratic participation in the country; half the population are denied the right to vote:

> The fewer the people who go to the polls—because they are illiterate, indifferent or absentee, or, because half the population constituted by the feminine elements is forbidden to vote . . . next will come the dictatorship of a few. The interests of a small group will silence the general yearnings.[5]

Amanda Labarca is the first Latin American woman to pursue a university professorship.

Sara Basterrechea Ramirez is a chemist in Guatemala and the sole woman faculty member of *Universidad de San Carlos*. Graciela Morales F. de Echeverria is an executive in Costa Rica's Social Security Office. Isabel Sánchez de Urdaneta is a teacher, active in the work of the Pan-American Union, and holds a diplomatic position for Venezuela in Washington.

Taking the lead for women's rights during the drafting of the Declaration alongside India and Latin America are the Soviet delegations to the United Nations. The male delegates in the Commission on Human Rights and the Third Committee will repeatedly propose amendments that strengthen the agenda endorsed by the Commission on the Status of Women to explicitly mention equality in the Declaration, such as their proposal for restating non-discrimination in several articles, as well as their support for equal pay.

Fryderyka Kalinowska, a translator and representative of Poland in the Commission on the Status of Women and in the Third Committee, will on several occasions support Soviet amendments to the Declaration that clearly state the responsibility and duties of the state to uphold human rights—especially economic rights. She will defend Soviet amendments that restrict the freedom of expression of fascists, as well as the Soviet's persistence in stating that human rights should be upheld by obligations of governments. Her arguments for repeating non-discrimination in several articles will be seconded by the Indian representative Lakshmi Menon.

In addition to Fryderyka Kalinowska, there are two other women who represent Soviet delegations in the Commission on the Status of Women; Elizavieta Alekseevna Popova of the Union of Soviet Socialist Republics, a lawyer and trade unionist, and Eydokia Uralova of the Byelorussian Soviet Socialist Republic, a history teacher and Senior Executive in the Ministry of Education.

The Soviet Union had been a forerunner of progressive legislation for women's rights in the early twentieth century when working-class women had led demonstrations for bread and peace, leading to the February Revolution in 1917. International Women's Day came to be celebrated in memory of these women's struggle. As leftist parties gained power following the Revolution, the Bolshevik government appointed its first female Minister, Alexandra Kollontai. As Social Minister, she introduced rights for women to own and inherit property, as well as the rights to divorce and have an abortion. There was, nonetheless, widespread resistance to prioritizing women's rights from male party colleagues whose main argument against such initiatives was that socialism, not feminism, should be at the forefront of the party politics and that female subjugation would be resolved once the issue of class was solved. As the Soviet Union moved toward communism under Stalin, the progressive laws for women that had been revolutionary at that time were reversed to conservative. The right to abortion was abolished in 1936, and a new family law made divorce difficult to obtain for women once again.

When the Commission on the Status of Women is established in the United Nations, the Soviet delegations are not forerunners of women's rights anymore, as fascism had silenced continuous demands for female emancipation from the 1930s onward.

Working more in the background during the drafting of the Declaration are the women delegates from China and the Middle East.

The Republic of China is represented by Xu Yizhen in the Sub-Commission on the Status of Women, nominated by Mr. Chang, delegate to the Commission on Human Rights, and by Cecilia Sieu-Ling Zung in the Commission on the Status of Women. The Chinese representatives work under pressured circumstances as their country is in the midst of a civil war. The nationalist and communist political parties in the Republic of China had only briefly joined forces against the Japanese invasion during the Second World War. In the years leading up to 1948, "For the first time in China's republican history, a small number of women leaders were appointed as council members by the Nationalist government."[6]

Women in the Republic of China had organized themselves through the Peking University Women (1920) and the Women's Advisory Committee (1938). Women in metropolitan Chongqing had insisted on a national unity government already in 1945. The National Assembly in the Republic of China holds direct elections from 21 January to 23 January 1948. The election takes three days as it involves around 200 million people, and over seven hundred representatives are elected from several political parties, including the Chinese Youth Party, the Chinese Democratic Socialist Party, the Communist Party of China, and the Nationalist Party. It is the largest democracy in the world in the postwar years through this direct election of legislative representation. In 1948, the first lady of China, Soong Mei-ling, is called the most powerful woman in the world by *Life Magazine*.

Cecilia Sieu-Ling Zung, delegate to the Commission on the Status of Women, is a graduate of Barnard College, where Virginia Gildersleeve is Dean. Cecilia Sieu-Ling is the author of *Secrets of the Chinese Drama* (1964).[7] She will stress the importance of delegations referring to the problems they are facing in the United Nations debates to avoid abstract discussions on the presumed perfection of national politics. Chair Marie-Hélène Lefaucheux will speak with esteem of her colleague in the Commission on the Status of Women: "As the representative of China [Cecilia Sieu-Ling Zung] sensibly and tactfully observed in our Commission, it would be more useful candidly to state a situation as it actually is and by common endeavor seek the best means of improving it."[8]

Xu Yizhen, delegate to the Sub-Commission on the Status of Women, had criticized the use of the wording 'brothers' in the draft Declaration. She will convey in an interview for the UN Status of Women Radio a few years later, "It has been said a woman's place is in the home. Before the public, the majority of women feel different of themselves."[9]

The Republic of China will be expelled from the United Nations after the Cold War, even though it was one of the founding members. Commenting on the women's active involvement in the war, Xu Yizhen says that, "During the last war, women working side by side with men have proven themselves by their achievements" and asks, "Why should women enslave themselves to tradition. Once they conquer this psychological weakness their status in society will be elevated."[10] Today, the Republic of China (Taiwan) has a democratically elected female President, Tsai Ing-wen.

Female delegates in the Commission on the Status of Women from the Middle East represent Lebanon (Angela Jurdak), Syria (Alice Kandalft Cosma), and Turkey (Mihri Pektas).

Angela Jurdak is Rapporteur to the Commission, nominated by Mr. Malik in the Commission on Human Rights. She holds a PhD in international relations from the American University in Washington, DC, and is the first woman instructor at the American University of Beirut and first woman diplomat of Lebanon. Alice Kandalft Cosma will be the following Rapporteur after Angela Jurdak to the Commission on the Status of Women. Alice Kandalft Cosma is Principal of the Doha National School of Damascus, a graduate of Teachers College, Columbia University. In 1939, she joined the Ministry of Education in Syria and was one of the organizers of the Arab Women's National League in Syria.

Europe and North America are represented by four Member States: Denmark (Bodil Begtrup), France (Marie-Hélène Lefaucheux), the United Kingdom (Mary Sutherland), and the United States (Dorothy Kenyon). Mary Sutherland is a leader in trade union activities in the United Kingdom and Chief Woman Officer of the Labour Party.

Suffragists found support beyond national borders and strength in the realization that women in other countries fought for similar issues: for peace, for suffrage, for human rights. Even though women had gained the right to vote in some democracies in Europe, they had not been able to actually use this right since the two World Wars created political instability and a state of emergency where regular democratic elections were not held.

An international arena like the United Nations, with the drafting of an international Declaration of rights, was the perfect place to advance the rights of women beyond borders—over national interests, through ideological barriers, and above religious conflicts: to make the rights of women an integral part of a universal concept of 'human rights.'

Mr. Humphrey writes in his memoirs, "more perhaps than any other United Nations body the delegates to the Commission on the Status of Women were personally committed to its objectives" as it "acted as a kind of lobby for the women of the world."[11]

## International Women's Lobby through Non-Governmental Organizations

The Commission on the Status of Women found itself far from alone in its determination to place women's rights on the international agenda in the United Nations. In response to the many sufferings resulting from the two World Wars, international women's organizations combined lobby work for women's rights with humanitarian activities. Initiatives were vast and included collaboration beyond borders to collect food supplies for soldiers, compiling cross-national signature lists for peace and disarmament, and sending children's clothing to Finland, Poland, and the Soviet Union to thousands of displaced children.

The women's organizations that lobby during the drafting of the Declaration will demand suffrage and rights for married women and will try to ensure that prostitution is included as a form of slavery or trafficking in the Declaration.

At the meetings of the Commission on the Status of Women in 1947, a hearing was granted to twelve international women's organizations with consultative status. International suffrage movements were represented at the hearing through the International Alliance of Women (AIW); the World Woman's Party (WWP); the International Council of Women (ICW) that represented fifty-three women's organizations from nine countries with Marie-Hélène Lefaucheux serving as President from 1957 to 1963; and the Women's International Democratic Federation (WIDF), an influential women's organization in postwar years that has been concerned with anti-fascism, world peace, child welfare, and improving the status of women.

Among them were also Christian and Protestant women's organizations that lobbied against trafficking and prostitution and for married women's rights. The World Young Women's Christian Association (YWCA) helped single working women moving from rural areas to London by offering housing, education, and support. The International Federation of Friends of Young Women, a Protestant association, assisted emigrating girls and women to prevent sexual exploitation. They documented traffic in women and girls after the Second World War for the purpose of prostitution or marriage. The World Women's Christian Temperance Union (WCTU) supported the Eighteenth Amendment to prohibit alcoholic beverages in the United States in order to create a 'sober and pure world' where women and children did not suffer from abuse, violence, and economic neglect in the home due to alcoholism. These organizations were combated by brewers' associations that funded anti-suffragist rallies.

At the Commission on the Status of Women hearing in 1947 were several women's organizations that worked to establish ties across borders to lobby for peace. Among them were the Associated Country Women of the World (ACWW); the Women's International League for Peace and Freedom; and the International Federation of University Women (IFUW) founded by Virginia Gildersleeve, Professor Caroline Spurgeon (University of London), and Rose Sidgwick (University of Birmingham) to unite university women around the world in fostering peace through friendship and understanding.

Organizations that lobbied for representation of women in leading positions, such as the International Federation of Business and Professional Women (IFBPW) and the Liaison Committee of Women's International Organization, have consultative status at the hearing. The latter is an international platform in which women from diverse organizations meet in a joint effort to support female representation internationally—in unions and government—as they had in the prior League of Nations.

The drafting committee under the Commission on Human Rights—in which Eleanor Roosevelt was the only female representative—received communications from several of these women's organizations. The International Alliance as well as the Associated Country Women of the World sends memorandums addressed to Eleanor Roosevelt requesting that points on women's rights be included in the bill of rights, drawing her attention to recommendations accepted at their respective conferences.

When the article on political rights (Article 21) is under debate in the Commission on Human Rights, the Commission on the Status of Women is backed by two international organizations—the International Council of Women and the International Union of Women's Catholic Organization—in its demand for universal suffrage for women. Bodil Begtrup suggests that the word "equal" be inserted before "election" in the article to state women's equal political rights. "In many countries," she notes, "suffrage is regulated by qualifications of class, income and sex."[12] Her proposal is encouraged by the International Council of Women (ICW), which "supports this view and emphasizes equality of suffrage."[13] The International Union of Women's Catholic Organization also supports this idea, stressing the "solidarity of women on the matter of equality of political rights,"[14] adding that "a comment should emphasize that the word 'everyone' in Article 21 contains no discrimination against women."[15]

Eydokia Uralova, Rapporteur, calls for equality to be recognized in the Article since without it "no real spirit of democracy can exist."[16] As it stands, Eydokia Uralova feels that the article "does not clearly define the rights of women."[17] She reminds the meeting that "women everywhere are looking to this Declaration as the recognition of their aspirations" and that campaigns against women's participation in public life should be condemned.[18]

The discussion on political rights raises many concrete challenges after the Second World War. In most countries, there exist different hindrances to women's suffrage; in the United States, the right to vote is coupled with requirements of property ownership; in the Soviet Union, only one party is expected to represent the people's interests—the Communist Party—in other countries, the roster of candidates on election day is limited to only one, rendering the right to vote something of a chimera. Estimates by UNESCO in 1947 rank adult illiteracy in the world at eighty-five percent.[19] (Seventy years later, in 2017, that number has been reversed—eighty-six percent of the adult population are literate according to numbers from UNESCO.)

The Commission on the Status of Women has approached several international women's organizations to assist in sending out questionnaires to states on the rights of women. Some have replied receptively, while others consider questionnaires unnecessary.[20] The lobby from Non-Governmental Organizations at the drafting of the Declaration is far from all pro-women's rights. The International Federation of Christian Trade Unions wishes to influence the wording in one of the most central articles of the Declaration;

namely, Article 3 on the right to life. Their representative, Mr. Vanistendael, asks for a specification "on when human life begins to protect life born or conceived."[21] He wishes the article to state that everyone has the right to life, personal liberty, and security "from the first moment of his physical development."[22] Bodil Begtrup responds that this cannot be reconciled with advanced legislation for the right of abortion.

The Commission on Human Rights adopts the text submitted by the Drafting Committee: "Everyone has the right to life, to personal liberty and to personal security."[23]

When Article 23 on the right to work is adopted in the Commission on Human Rights, with the formulation that "Women shall have the right to work under the same conditions as men, and to receive equal pay for equal work," Eleanor Roosevelt urges the women's organizations to carefully consider the demand on women during the pre-natal period and other aspects of the formulation "same conditions as men" to ensure the protection of women.[24] The article is adopted with the reservation of the protection of women for insertion later in the article.[25]

The focus in the debate regarding the right to work is initially not on equal pay for equal work but rather on the duties of the state to primarily ensure the opportunity to work, as the unemployment rate was high in the postwar years. Mr. Cassin of France suggests the following wording: "The State has a duty to take such measures as may be within its powers to ensure that all its citizens have an opportunity for useful work."[26] Eleanor Roosevelt points out that the state might not be able to provide useful work for everyone.

Mr. Romulo of the Philippines proposes a new text to the article, which includes "Women shall have the right to work under the same conditions as men and to receive equal pay for equal work."[27] Eydokia Uralova of the Commission on the Status of Women endorses the proposal. "The right to work and to pay is of particular importance to women engaged in public employment where men are still receiving far higher rates than women"[28] she affirms. At this point, a clear reference to non-discrimination of women in the article is not yet rendered.

The principle of a "basic wage" in Australia was a contemporary example of unequal pay, a wage-system "built on the assumption that every man needs a wage sufficient to provide for the basic needs of a family unit of himself, a wife and three children."[29] Jessie Street recalls, "The basic wage was the bastion of unequal pay, as it applied to male workers whether single or married, fathers or childless, while female workers were entitled only to 54 per cent of the male wage regardless of their dependents."[30]

Jessie Street had experienced that male colleagues in the Australian delegation were paid more for the same appointment. She recalls in her memoirs from the San Francisco Conference:

> They had been buying all sorts of things for themselves as well as presents to take back since they arrived and I had wondered how they

> managed. When they asked me what I had been spending my delegate's allowance on, I told them how much I was getting. I then found they were receiving about three times as much as I was.[31]

She was furious about this inequality and demanded from the official who had made the arrangements to be compensated. Minerva Bernardino had a similar experience from governmental work in the Dominican Republic as she had not been given a due raise alongside promotion—with the explanation from her superior that Dominican women could not earn more than men did.[32]

When the question of equal pay is debated in the Commission on Human Rights, Eydokia Uralova reminds the male delegates of the added unfairness in employment for women as, frequently, public appointments are kept open until a man is accepted.[33] According to Eydokia Uralova, not only are the right to equal pay and to employment necessary but the equal right to benefits in employment are required, too. The 1937 report from the League of Nations emphasized the aspect of equality in the right to work, pay and leisure. Eydokia Uralova proposes that the wording of this report can be used in the Declaration.[34] This proposal will be taken up again by representatives of the Commission on the Status of Women when the Declaration is debated in the Third Committee.

## Notes

1. Interview with Begum Hamid Ali. Lake Success, January 1949, UN Status of Women Radio Division, 1.
2. Social Affairs Registry, *Human Rights Division—Miscellaneous* (New York: Committee on Status of Women, February 1947), November 12, 1946–April 21, 1947. Letters from Humphrey to female delegates for the first session on the Commission on the Status of Women, December 27, 1946.
3. Ibid.
4. Bodil Begtrup, Denmark is Chair of the Sub-Commission. The other delegates in the Sub-Commission are: Xu Yizhen, China; Minerva Bernardino, Dominican Republic; Hansa Mehta, India; Marie-Hélène Lefaucheux, France; Angela Jurdak, Lebanon; and Fryderyka Kalinowska, Poland.
5. Amanda Labarca, "Trayectoria Del Movimiento Feminista de Chile," in *Feminismo Contemporéno* (Chile: Zig-Zag, 1947), 139.
6. Danke Li, *Echoes of Chongqing: Women in Wartime China* (United States: University of Illinois Press, 2010), 9.
7. Cecilia Sieu Ling Zung, *Secrets of the Chinese Drama: A Complete Explanatory Guide to Actions and Symbols as Seen in the Performance of Chinese Dramas* (New York: Arno Press, 1964).
8. Lefaucheux, "Work for Women's Equality of Status," 343.
9. Interview with Mrs. New. Lake Success, January 1949, UN Status of Women Radio Division, 1.
10. Ibid.
11. Humphrey cited in Linder, "Equality for Women," 186.
12. Working Group on the Declaration of Human Rights, summary record 7th meeting, December 9, 1947, E/CN.4/AC.2/SR.7, 9.

13. Ibid.
14. Ibid., 10.
15. Ibid., 10.
16. Ibid., 9.
17. Ibid., 9.
18. Ibid., 10.
19. Third Committee, summary record 133rd meeting, November 12, 1948, A/C.3/SR.133, 466.
20. Commission on the Status of Women, summary record of the 9th meeting, New York, February 14, 1947, E/CN.6/SR.9, 5.
21. Working Group on the Declaration of Human Rights, summary record 3rd meeting, December 6, 1947, E/CN.4/AC.2/SR.3, 7.
22. Ibid.
23. Ibid., 8.
24. Working Group on the Declaration of Human Rights, summary record 7th meeting, December 9, 1947, E/CN.4/AC.2/SR.7, 14.
25. Ibid.
26. Ibid., 12.
27. Ibid., 13.
28. Ibid., 13.
29. Street, *Truth or Repose*, 93.
30. Ibid., 93–94.
31. Ibid., 184.
32. Bernardino, "Introduction," *Lucha, Agonía y Esperanza*, xxii.
33. Working Group on the Declaration of Human Rights, summary record 7th meeting, December 9, 1947, E/CN.4/AC.2/SR.7, 13.
34. Status of Women. *Report Submitted by the First Committee to the Assembly.* Official No. A.54.1937.V (Geneva: League of Nations, 1937).

# 6 A Lack of Acknowledgment

## 'Men' Trumps 'All Human Beings'

> Let our women realize themselves that it is we who are the builders; it is we who supply manpower and womanpower, day after day, year after year, country after country. Do we get any acknowledgement? No. Are countries and governments grateful? No.[1]
>
> —Begum Hamid Ali, India

The Declaration, one year into the drafting process under the Commission on Human Rights, is still addressing 'all men' and not 'everyone.' In November and December 1947, the Commission on Human Rights and the Commission on the Status of Women are convening in *Palais de Nations*, Geneva, Switzerland. *Palais de Nations* is an impressive white building located in a beautiful park on Lake Geneva, which was built as the headquarters of the former League of Nations. With Swedish marble columns separated by nine massive bay windows stretching from floor to ceiling, its location on the Ariana hillside overlooking the lake was breath-taking. It had been the first Secretary-General of the League of Nations Eric Drummond who had insisted on its view of the snow-clad mountain peaks of Mount Blanc. *Palais de Nations* has become known as the 'heart of the United Nations human rights work.' Still 'human rights' are referred to as '*droits de l'homme*' in French, something that the Commission on the Status of Women will question, suggesting instead '*droits de l'homme et femme.*'

The two commissions convening in Geneva are to consider the report from the Sub-Commission on the Prevention of Discrimination and Protection of Minorities. What is to be defined as discrimination and what is not is a question raised in debates on the non-discrimination list in the Declaration.

### Do Women's Rights Fit in a Footnote?

When women's rights were first discussed in the Commission on Human Rights, the immediate response by male delegates had been to insert a footnote stating that all rights applied to women as well. A footnote, however, is not what the Commission on the Status of Women has envisioned as the rightful place in the Declaration for stating the equal rights of women. "The drafting of a Declaration on Human Rights is of fundamental importance for women, who in certain countries are not even granted the rights which the most primitive constitutions granted to men,"[2] announces Chair of the Commission on the Status of Women Bodil Begtrup at the second meeting of the working group on the Declaration in December 1947.

A rather strange debate will follow in the working group to the Commission on Human Rights as the Chair of the Commission on the Status of Women tries to lift the importance of including women in the Declaration, while the Chair of the Commission on Human Rights tries to move past these interruptions in the discussions, and the male delegates simply continue debating the expressions "all men are brothers" and "members of one family" in the Declaration.

Bodil Begtrup is of the conviction that "as sex equality is a right which had been acquired but recently, it will be necessary to emphasize it explicitly in certain articles, and even, to make particular mention of certain rights granted specially to women."[3] Therefore, she proposes that:

> [T]he following text be inserted in the Preamble: "When a word indicating the masculine sex is used in connection with a provision contained in the following Bill of Human Rights, the provision in question is to be considered as applying without discrimination to women."[4]

Without responding to this suggestion by the Commission on the Status of Women, Eleanor Roosevelt suggests that the meeting moves on to examine each article of the draft.

While examining Article 1, Mr. Romulo disputes its reasoning: "There is no logical connection between the two parts of the sentence 'Being endowed with reason and conscience, they are members of one family'."[5] To remedy the disjuncture, he proposes the following draft: "All men are brothers. Being endowed with reason and conscience, they are free and possess equal dignity and rights."[6]

Bodil Begtrup insists that it will "be preferable to substitute the term 'human beings' for the term 'men'," used in the Declaration. Eleanor Roosevelt responds that this is "rather a question of translation affecting the French text."[7]

Mr. Amado of Panama feels the expression "members of one family" is religious or philosophical and does not express the fundamental principles of the Declaration.[8] He is seconded by Mr. Bogomolov of the USSR. Mr. Cassin of France explains that the drafters had wished to "indicate the unity of the human race regardless of frontiers, as opposed to theories like those of Hitler."[9] To meet this last criticism of the wording "members of one family" in Article 1, Mr. Cassin suggests that it could be said only that "men should refrain from inciting hatred."[10]

*Figure 6.1* Marie-Hélène Lefaucheux, French representative on the Commission on the Status of Women, 12 February 1947, Lake Success, New York.

Credit: UN Photo.

Rapporteur of the Commission on the Status of Women Eydokia Uralova conceives the terms in which the article is drafted "too high-flown to be easily understandable by all." She also thinks that "the equality of the sexes should be more clearly stated."[11]

The critical observations by the representatives from the Commission on the Status of Women on the draft are at this instance not heeded by the male delegates in the working group. Stating equality of the sexes in Article 1 is not decided on before the meeting is over. Mr. Cassin of France is given the task of re-drafting the article to respond to the male delegates' concerns.

## Lefaucheux—Non-discrimination in Article 2

The new Chair of the Commission on the Status of Women, Marie-Hélène Lefaucheux, writes in the United Nations Bulletin about the Commission's work in the United Nations: "The habit so dear to some delegates, of dwelling complacently on the perfections of the systems in their own countries in reference to any subject brought up is not very constructive."[12]

Active in the French Resistance during the Second World War, Marie-Hélène Lefaucheux served as Vice-Chair of the Paris branch of the French Committee of National Liberation. After the war, she becomes one of few women to receive the *Croix de Guerre*. She serves as Deputy to the Constituent Assembly of France in 1945 and is elected to the first Council of the French Fourth Republic in 1946 after the adoption of the new constitution.

When the Declaration is drafted (1946–48), women in France had had the right to vote in only one election on 29 April 1945. Born two hundred years before women in France could finally vote in national elections, the French playwright Olympe de Gouges (1746–93) writes a Declaration on the Rights of Woman and Female Citizen (*la Déclaration de droites de la Femme et de la Citoyenne*)—a critical response to the French Declaration of the Rights of Man and the Citizen (*le Déclaration de Droites de L'homme et du Cityoen*). In her pamphlet, Olympe de Gouges asserts that French women should be included as rights bearers. In response to her argument on women's rights, she is seen as a threat to the state and is killed by guillotine in 1793 amid the French Revolution. The French Revolution brought liberty, equality, and fraternity amongst *men*—a revolt against an elite in order to include more *men* in the definition of *du cityoen*. Olympe de Gouges' death is a testimony in itself to the claim she had furthered in the Declaration on the Rights of Woman and the Female Citizen. Since women in France could be prosecuted as enemies of the state, it seemed they were regarded as political subjects; as political subjects, they should also have political rights and political freedom. If a person can pose a threat in a national court, she should be seen as a subject in the French Assembly, too, where the laws under which she can be sentenced have been drafted and adopted.

One hundred years after Olympe de Gouges was killed for expressing that women should be part of fraternity, another French woman, Hubertine Auclert (born in 1848), was eligibly the first woman to call herself a *feminist* and also dedicated her life to bringing liberty and equality to women. Hubertine Auclert became the leader of the militant suffragette movement *Société le droit des femmes*, founded in 1876. The movement was later renamed *Société le suffrage des femmes* and started the magazine *La Citoyenne*, which focused on women's rights to education, to divorce, and to economic independence. With time, the magazine placed increased emphasis on women's right to vote in France.

The same rights that had been championed by women in the middle of the 1800s are now debated in the middle of the 1900s in the United Nations—will 'human rights' be formulated more progressively than the historical 'Rights of Man'? The representation by the Commission on the Status of Women, with at least three delegates to the debates on the Declaration, will not go unnoticed. Marie-Hélène Lefaucheux will make sure that protection against sex discrimination is mentioned in the list of non-discrimination of Article 2.

When Mr. Malik calls for a vote on Article 2, he is interrupted by a representative of the Commission on the Status of Women—Marie-Hélène Lefaucheux.[13] The Commission on Human Rights is voting on the third part of the Soviet delegate Mr. Borisov's text on non-discrimination. Mr. Borisov's text reads: "Any action establishing a privilege or a discrimination based on distinctions of race, nationality or religion constitutes a crime."[14] Marie-Hélène Lefaucheux feels that "the omission of the word 'sex' is due to an oversight on Mr. Borisov's part." Mr. Malik thanks Marie-Hélène Lefaucheux "for her remark and takes the opportunity to express his satisfaction at the presence among the members of a representative of the Commission on the Status of Women."[15]

Mr. Borisov remarks that it is "merely a question of drafting and that he has no objection to inserting the word 'sex,' since by virtue of the first paragraph, the provisions of the second paragraph should be understood as applying equally to women."[16] At this point, the delegate of Haiti, Mr. Roy, has to "raise a point of order, in view of the demurs voiced by some members."[17]

That the United Nations records mention the demurs voiced by some members is an indication that the suggestion that all rights apply equally to women is a controversial idea when, finally, women have a say in international politics.

Chair Marie-Hélène Lefaucheux prefers the work in her Commission to focus on changes to be made in the Declaration and not to worry itself too much with gaining support from other bodies in the United Nations. As the Commission on the Status of Women has from the outset been looked upon skeptically by the Chair of the Commission on Human Rights—as superfluous in the organization since there are already 'experts' on human rights—Marie-Hélène Lefaucheux wants to make sure that the changes they advocate speak for themselves in making 'human rights' inclusive. In the United Nations Bulletin in 1949, Marie-Hélène Lefaucheux reflects on the pros with this approach:

> [T]he affairs of the various Councils or Commissions of the United Nations, and of the specialized agencies or non-governmental organizations, are not always of such direct concern to us. . . . First we must work, carry out a definite task, seek concrete results; and then, in proportion to their own efficiency, the other wheels of the great international machine will serve our activity as we shall serve theirs.[18]

One of the initial opponents to a full Commission on the Status of Women, American delegate Dorothy Kenyon, a former New York City Municipal Court Justice, will quote in 1953 the UN Charter on "non-discrimination based on sex" when asking if this kind of phrasing could not be used instead of the Equal Rights Amendment.[19]

*Figure 6.2* Isabel de Urdaneta, Venezuela, and Dorothy Kenyon, the United States. Second Session of the Commission on the Status of Women, 5 January 1948, Lake Success, New York.

Credit: UN Photo/Kari Berggrav.

## Article 1—'All Men' Trumps 'All Human Beings'

It is December 1947 in Geneva when the Commission returns to Article 1 of the Declaration.[20] The discussion is initiated by a dissenting voice from India. Hansa Mehta says she does "not like the wording 'all men' or 'and should act towards one another like brothers,' she feels they might be interpreted to exclude women, and are out of date."[21]

Eleanor Roosevelt replies that "the word 'men' used in this sense is generally accepted to include all human beings."[22]

Mr. Duke suggests that:

> [I]n order to avoid further discussion on the subject, a note should be included at the beginning of both Documents [draft to the Declaration and a Convention] to the effect that the word 'men,' as used therein, refers to all human beings.[23]

Hansa Mehta makes known that she "has no objection to the United Kingdom suggestion, but Article 1 is the only place in the Declaration where the expression 'men' appears. She wishes to have this changed to 'human beings' or 'persons'."[24]

A discussion follows as to the advisability of: 1) accepting the alteration suggested by the Indian representative; 2) inserting a footnote to Article 1; or 3) adopting the proposal of the United Kingdom representative that simply states 'all men.'

A vote is taken on the text with the formulation 'all men,' and Article 1 is adopted twelve votes to zero, with five abstentions.[25]

## The Declaration Needs to Be Easily Understood

The resistance toward using a more inclusive wording in the Declaration, such as 'human beings,' is coupled with a more general debate on whether the Commission on Human Rights is actually drafting a Declaration of 'human rights' or on 'the rights of states.' Mr. Hodgson of Australia enquires later in the meeting "why the Declaration is limited to 'persons',"[26] and he proposes that the phrase 'right of any State or any person' be used.[27]

Hansa Mehta points out that "the Declaration deals with the rights of individuals and not of States."[28]

Mr. Malik of Lebanon concurs that "the observation of the representative of India is strictly correct, but he has no objection if the Australian representative wishes the rights of Governments to be included."[29]

The distinction between the rights of governments versus that of individuals in the Declaration is of utmost importance as it defines the main purpose of the United Nations organization. Will it be to protect the interests of governments to its Member States for the sake of peace through international diplomacy? Or will it be to protect the rights of people against oppression and human rights atrocities by governments to its Member States?

Mr. Cassin of France, who has been working with the initial draft, observes that in the Declaration under consideration, the Commission is "bound to emphasize the rights of man as an individual as opposed to the universal rights of nations."[30] This sets the Declaration apart from the UN Charter, as the Charter covers the rights and duties of Member States, such as the right to sovereignty and the duty to adhere to decisions made by the Security Council. The Charter establishes the main functions of the organization: to establish long lasting peace between nations and to respect and safeguard 'human rights' in the world, though the numeration of these rights is to be defined in the subsequent document—the Declaration.

The Commission on Human Rights will be drawing up two documents to be prepared for the Third Committee; a non-legally binding Declaration and a Convention that will be legally binding upon ratification. Now the educational aim of the Declaration—for everyone to know their rights—becomes more urgent as the realization of these rights depends on a widespread knowledge of what they are. The text is to be read and understood by 'ordinary people.' In the Commission on Human Rights, Hansa Mehta is supported in her view that the Declaration needs to be short, simple, and easy to understand. She is convinced that if the Declaration is disseminated among the populace, it will influence legislation in many countries. Even though she is critical of the wording in several articles—they are not drafted to be 'operationalized' through direct legislation—she explains in her book *Indian Woman* that the Constituent Assembly of India, under her influence, was taking inspiration from the rights in the Declaration:

> I had the privilege being one of the few women who were members of the Constituent Assembly and of working on the sub-committee on 'Fundamental Rights,' along with the late Rajkumari Amrit Kaur who was the first Woman Cabinet Minister. The sub-committee had before it the Declaration of Human Rights passed by the General Assembly of the United Nations in 1948.[31]

Hansa Mehta had been member to the Bombay Legislative Council, under British administration in 1931, and after independence she is one of few women members of the Constituent Assembly of India. The wording in the document will have far greater importance than some of the Western delegates might have perceived.

*Figure 6.3* Bodil Begtrup, Denmark, with Graciela Morales F. de Echeverria, Costa Rica, Second Session of the Commission on the Status of Women, 20 January 1948, Lake Success, New York.

Credit: UN Photo/Kari Berggrav.

## In a Spirit of Sisterhood

In January 1948, the Commission on the Status of Women is back at Lake Success in New York, in the building with its huge, oval-shaped driveway, the flags of the Member States fly atop the now fifty-seven poles in the windy fields surrounding the Sperry Gyroscope Plant. The members of the Commission on the Status of Women meet to summarize their efforts from attending the Human Rights Commission meetings in Geneva in December 1947 and to focus their energies for the upcoming May and June meetings of the Commission on Human Rights in New York. The forthcoming summer sessions will be the last instance when the Commission on the Status of Women can influence the work of the Commission on Human Rights directly, after which it will retain some continued leverage through its representatives in the Third Committee.

Bodil Begtrup summarizes their journey thus far. She finds it "difficult to participate in debates over the Declaration without having a vote or the right to propose a motion, as the members of the Commission on Human Rights have."[32] The representatives of the Commission on the Status of Women can only express wishes. In many instances in the text of the Declaration, the expression 'his' and 'him' is used. "This has been brought up by the representatives of the Commission on the Status of Women as expressions of a language excluding women."[33] A note in the preamble has been suggested—that 'his' or 'him' should not be understood as implying discrimination of women.[34] 'His' and 'him' are by this note supposed to apply to women, too. The words 'all men are brothers' has been criticized by several members of the Commission on the Status of Women as furthering an old-fashioned notion and, since outdated, should be replaced with a new phrase that better reflects the new world.

Article 2 on non-discrimination, as it now includes sex, is more inclusive of women's rights as it must be read to cover "also the discriminatory treatment of prostitutes or women presumed to be prostitutes,"[35] reasons Bodil Begtrup. The Commission on the Status of Women has been assured by the Commission on Human Rights that Article 4[36] that prohibits slavery is meant to prohibit trafficking of women and children.[37]

The most critical article in the current draft, she concludes, seems to be Article 16[38] on the rights in marriage "as it does not mention specifically equal freedom in respect of the dissolution of marriage."[39] Bodil Begtrup has suggested the inclusion of a clause ensuring "full equality in all civil rights, irrespective of marriage, nationality, race, language or religion."[40]

Regarding advances in the Declaration, paragraph two of Article 23 on the right to work, which reads: "Women shall work with the same advantages as men and receive equal pay for equal work,"[41] can be credited, acknowledges Bodil Begtrup, to a large extent to Eydokia Uralova, who has made a strong plea for the equality of economic and social rights between men and women.[42]

In retrospect, Bodil Begtrup explicates that the experience gained by attending the last session of the Commission on Human Rights shows "the importance of having a representative of the Commission attend the debates of drafting groups"[43]—any change they wish to advocate should be presented as a recommendation to the Economic and Social Council.

Following this summary of the Commission's observations of the drafting process so far, Jessie Street comments on the prevailing use of 'man' in the Declaration. She prefers the Commission to suggest a comment in the Declaration stating that wherever the word 'man' is used, it implies both men and women. She points out that:

> [A]lthough the text obviously includes women, this terminology has been interpreted restrictively in the past so that women have had to wage a constant fight to secure the same rights as men for voting, university education and access to liberal professions.[44]

Dorothy Kenyon thinks that the term 'persons' can be used in Article 1 or 'people' as appears in the Charter, instead of the word 'man,' but she is against "the inclusion of explanatory sentences in the Declaration." Along the same argumentative lines as the male delegates in the Commission on Human Rights, she reasons that it would be better as a footnote or comment.[45]

Bodil Begtrup points out that stating in Article 1 that 'all men are born free and equal in rights and dignity' "provides the wrong start for a Declaration in which equality between men and women is to be expressed."[46]

Cecilia Sieu-Ling Zung of China postulates that "the idea of equality of women and men will be best expressed in a sub-heading to the title of the Declaration."[47]

This proposal is not elaborated on further by the other members of the Commission on the Status of Women, so there is no suggestion of how this would have been expressed in a sub-heading to the Declaration. The Commission decides by seven votes to replace the term 'man' in the Declaration by a more general term.[48]

Cecilia Sieu-Ling Zung calls for "the term 'brothers' used in Article 1 to be replaced by some more general term like 'members of the same family'."[49] Begum Hamid Ali offers 'in a spirit of brotherhood'[50] as an alternative. After some deliberation as to whether 'in a spirit of brotherhood and sisterhood' would not preserve equality still better, "the Commission feels that the 'spirit of brotherhood' sufficiently expresses the idea advocated."[51]

By a majority of twelve votes, the Commission decides to recommend that the words "and should act toward one another like brothers" appearing at the end of Article 1 should be changed to "and should act toward one another in a spirit of brotherhood."[52]

The article on non-discrimination is at this point in the drafting process placed after the article on liberty and security of person, and "some

*Figure 6.4* Begum Hamid Ali, India, talks to Eydokia Uralova, the Byelorussian SSR, and her interpreter. Second Session of the Commission on the Status of Women, 5 January 1948, Lake Success, New York.

Credit: UN Photo/Kari Berggrav.

of the delegates feel that if Article 3 [in the final version Article 2 on non-discrimination] is to appear as two the emphasis on equality will be enhanced."[53] This is also what ultimately occurs.

## Explicit Mention of Divorce in the Declaration

The Commission on the Status of Women has several suggestions for amendments to Article 16 on marriage. Jessie Street wants the article to mention equal rights to divorce.[54] Begum Hamid Ali wishes monogamy to also be included in the article. There is no consensus in the Commission on the Status of Women regarding non-discrimination in relation to marriage. For example, Dorothy Kenyon does not consider women's right to nationality when contracting marriage as a matter of discrimination against women.[55]

Jessie Street proposes that Article 16 on rights in marriage should "contain some provisions for divorce as in some countries women can be divorced on the slightest pretext where in others a divorce is practically unobtainable for them."[56] The difficulty for women to obtain a divorce can have many unseen and damaging effects for women and children, as Jessie Street has observed through her political activism.

Jessie Street has volunteered with an organization formed to respond to the needs of families of those enlisted in the Australian Army. She was responsible for a district in which she went from door to door to collect information on families' needs. As she asked a woman with several small children, "Are you married?" the woman answered, "No fear."[57] Jessie Street was puzzled by this answer, but the women she visited in the working-class neighborhood testified that, "If I was married to him he could beat me," or "If I married him I couldn't leave him."[58] The Australian law regarding marriage did not allow women to divorce if beaten and left them without a say in the family's economic management. Had these women married, they could have lost the right to decide how to spend their own salary, the right to continue working, and safety for themselves and their children. The women explained that they needed at least to have their own salary for their kids to survive—something not secured through marriage.

Begum Hamid Ali supports the motion of Jessie Street of Australia and in addition to this "wants the Commission to support the principle of monogamy, as proclaimed in parts of India."[59] Begum Hamid Ali proposes the following resolution: "The Commission on the Status of Women expresses its belief in the principle of monogamy and advocates its acceptance by the United Nations."[60]

A discussion arises within the Commission on the Status of Women over whether to insert in Article 16 on marriage the right to nationality. Dorothy Kenyon wants the Declaration to "follow the broad pattern of the United States Bill of Rights, defining first the duties of the state toward the individual and protection of the individual from possible tyrannical acts by the state."[61] She thinks that "the family should be explicitly protected against the state,"[62] and that women's right to nationality when contracting marriage is "not in fact a matter of discrimination against women, so that the Commission is not empowered to deal with that subject."[63]

The Commission on the Status of Women, nonetheless, urges the Economic and Social Council to consider "Full equality in all civil rights, irrespective of nationality, race, language or religion, including (a) *Marriage*—Freedom of choice, dignity of the wife, monogamy, equal right to dissolution of marriage."[64]

Why should a woman lose her nationality when getting married if men did not? Was this not a case of discrimination? As in so many other issues related to women's legal status and social security, women were often socially pressured to exchange their dignity and rights through marriage or prostitution for economic survival or security. At this time, married women in many countries had less rights than single women, and certain employments were not open to married women, who were expected to become housewives. Sweden had sent a report to the Commission on the Status of Women on the condition of married women, in the hope that these inequalities would be brought to the attention of the United Nations.

## Notes

1. Interview with Begum Hamid Ali. Lake Success, January 1949, UN Status of Women Radio Division, 1.
2. Working Group on the Declaration of Human Rights, summary record 2nd meeting, December 5, 1947, E/CN.4/AC.2/SR.2, 2.
3. Ibid., 2–3.
4. Ibid., 3.
5. Ibid., 4.
6. Ibid., 4.
7. Ibid., 4.
8. Ibid., 4.
9. Ibid., 5.
10. Ibid., 6.
11. Ibid., 5.
12. Lefaucheux, "Work for Women's Equality of Status," 343.
13. Commission on the Prevention of Discrimination and Protection of Minorities, summary record 8th meeting, November 28, 1947, E/CN.4/Sub.2/SR.8, 12 (consideration of the second paragraph of Mr. Borisov's opinion on article 6).
14. Commission on the Prevention of Discrimination and Protection of Minorities, summary record 8th meeting, 28 November 1947, E/CN.4/Sub.2/SR.8, 12.
15. Ibid.
16. Ibid.
17. Ibid.
18. Lefaucheux, "Work for Women's Equality of Status," 343.
19. "Equal Rights for Women," by Dorothy Kenyon, *Civil Liberties*, April 1953.
20. Universal Declaration of Human Rights, Article 1; All human beings are born free and equal in dignity and rights. They are endowed with reason and conscience and should act towards one another in a spirit of brotherhood.
21. Commission on Human Rights, summary record 34th meeting, December 12, 1947, E/CN.4/SR.34, E/CN.4/57, 4.
22. Ibid.
23. Ibid.
24. Ibid.
25. Ibid.
26. Commission on Human Rights, summary record 41st meeting, December 16, 1947, E/CN.4/SR.41, 8.
27. Ibid.
28. Ibid.
29. Ibid.
30. Commission on Human Rights, summary record 7th meeting, January 31, 1947, E/CN.4/SR.7, 5.
31. Mehta, *Indian Woman*, 91.
32. Commission on the Status of Women, summary record 9th meeting, January 9, 1948, E/CN.6/SR.28, 2.
33. Ibid.
34. "When a noun or pronoun denoting the male sex is used in respect of any provision contained in the Bill of Human Rights, such provision shall apply without discrimination to the female sex."
35. Commission on the Status of Women, summary record 9th meeting, January 9, 1948, E/CN.6/SR.28, 2.
36. Article 4; No one shall be held in slavery or servitude; slavery and the slave trade shall be prohibited in all their forms.
37. Commission on the Status of Women, summary record 9th meeting, January 9, 1948, E/CN.6/SR.28, 3.

38. Article 16; 1. Men and women of full age, without any limitation due to race, nationality or religion, have the right to marry and to found a family. They are entitled to equal rights as to marriage, during marriage and at its dissolution. 2. Marriage shall be entered into only with the free and full consent of the intending spouses. 3. The family is the natural and fundamental group unit of society and is entitled to protection by society and the State.
39. Commission on the Status of Women, summary record 9th meeting, January 9, 1948, E/CN.6/SR.28, 3.
40. Ibid.
41. Article 23; 2. Everyone, without any discrimination, has the right to equal pay for equal work.
42. Commission on the Status of Women, summary record 9th meeting, January 9, 1948, E/CN.6/SR.28, 3.
43. Ibid., 4.
44. Ibid., 4.
45. Ibid., 4–5.
46. Ibid., 5.
47. Ibid., 5.
48. Ibid., 5.
49. Ibid., 5.
50. Ibid., 5.
51. Ibid., 5.
52. Ibid., 5
53. Ibid., 5.
54. Ibid., 7.
55. Ibid., 6.
56. Ibid., 7.
57. Street, *Truth or Repose*, 43.
58. Ibid., 43.
59. Commission on the Status of Women, summary record 9th meeting, January 9, 1948, E/CN.6/SR.28, 7.
60. Ibid., 6.
61. Ibid., 6.
62. Ibid., 6.
63. Ibid., 6.
64. Commission on the Status of Women, draft report of the Commission on the Status of Women to the Economic and Social Council, January 15, 1948, E/CN.6/74, 14.

# 7 The Commission on Human Rights Pressured to Consider the Rights of Women

> As men are organizing themselves, either fundamentally or by contribution to defend their countries, so let you and me and every woman join hands to give the best we have for education, health, civics, and above all, for peace.[1]
>
> —Begum Hamid Ali, India

The two Commissions under the Economic and Social Council—one mainly focused on 'the Rights of Man,' the other with a mandate to voice 'the rights of women'—move into the last phase of intense negotiations over wording in the Declaration in May 1948. This last summer in New York at Lake Success, the respective Chairs Eleanor Roosevelt and Marie-Hélène Lefaucheux did not have to worry that meetings would be held up without transport as had been the case during some of their earlier snowy winter sessions at the Sperry Plant, while those delegates intended to take part in the Third Committee meetings after the summer can look forward to spending the fall of 1948 in Paris.

When the issue of whether the wording of 'all men' is inclusive or not is up for debate again, on 28 May 1948, the Commission on Human Rights has held over fifty meetings. Hansa Mehta introduces the draft Declaration, submitted jointly by her delegation and that of the United Kingdom.[2] It is ten days after the United Kingdom delegate Mr. Dukes' sudden death and his replacement in the Commission on Human Rights by Mr. Wilson. Can this loss of a colleague with whom all had worked in the Commission on Human Rights have influenced the shift of support to the text that had been prepared by the two delegations?

Hansa Mehta explains that "the draft Declaration of the Drafting Committee has been criticized as being too long, and containing several irrelevant matters." She thinks "the Chinese draft is too terse. The French draft, on the other hand, while having a human appeal," according to Hansa Mehta "goes into too many details."[3]

Mr. Wilson associates himself "wholeheartedly with the statement of Hansa Mehta. If the Declaration is to reach the greatest possible number of people, it is essential for it to be expressed in the simplest terms."[4]

Will Hansa Mehta's persistence in seeking a more gender-equal wording in Article 1 of the Declaration finally gain majority support in the Commission on Human Rights?

## Article 1—Revisited

It has taken fifty meetings of heated debate in the Commission on Human Rights when Eleanor Roosevelt at last supports Hansa Mehta's proposal with its "minor drafting changes"—namely, "all people, men and women" in place of "all men" and "in the spirit of brotherhood" in place of "like brothers."

Eleanor Roosevelt explains that she is convinced that "discrimination against women has no place in the laws of any State."[5] She wishes to "make it clear, however, that equality does not mean identical treatment for men and women in all matters; there are certain cases, as for example the case of maternity benefits, where differential treatment is essential."[6]

There seems, for the first time, to be an agreement in the Commission that the wording "all men" is out of date. Nevertheless, there is some divergence on the best wording to replace the initial 'all men' in Article 1 of the Declaration. The Commission on the Status of Women, represented by its Vice-Chair Amalia Castillo de Ledón of Mexico, supports the Indian suggestion: "all people, men and women." Mr. Lebeau of Belgium prefers "all human beings," whereas the French delegation suggests "all members of the human family."

The argument against explicitly mentioning "men and women" is put forward as "simply" an issue of translation, and once again the French language is referenced in demonstrating how "absurd" it would sound to mention women, *"tous les hommes, hommes et femmes"*—although the French delegation now agrees with the criticism of "all men."[7]

Amalia de Castillo Ledón evokes that at its session in January 1948, the Commission on the Status of Women decided unanimously to request the Economic and Social Council to refer to the Commission on Human Rights the following amendments to Article 1 of the draft Declaration: "The words 'all people' should be substituted for 'all men,' and 'in a spirit of brotherhood' for 'like brothers'."[8] She says that her Commission realizes that 'all men' may *sound* general, but it has a "certain ambiguity" to it, so it would be preferable to use the wording from the preamble of the UN Charter.

Mr. Santa Cruz of Chile supports the suggestion made by Amalia de Castillo Ledón. He thinks that the "conclusion drawn in Article 1 that men should act towards one another in a spirit of brotherhood because they are endowed by nature with reason and conscience"[9] is a statement that should be open to debate. This is the wording that Mr. Romulo had suggested in earlier meetings of the Commission in critique of the French wording "members of the human family."

Mr. Cassin replies that "the French delegation has been conscious of the criticism which might be leveled at the words 'all men' and has therefore used the expression 'all members of the human family' in its draft of Article 1."[10] That expression he thinks is "all-inclusive" and stresses "the inherent equality of human beings, a concept which has recently been attacked by Hitler and his ideological disciples."[11]

Mr. Lebeau supports the French draft of Article 1, as he thinks "the expression 'all people, men and women' used in the Indian-United Kingdom text will sound absurd if translated into French,"[12] ['*tous les hommes, hommes et femmes*']. He feels that in trying to accentuate the idea of equality, the result is quite the opposite and creates the impression of discrimination.[13] The words 'all men' used in the Drafting Committee's text are preferable in his opinion, "for that formula has been used in countless declarations in the past."[14] He sees that a compromise can be reached if Article 1 is to start with the words 'all human beings.'[15]

Hansa Mehta wishes to "hear the opinion of the representative of the Commission on the Status of Women"[16] Amalia de Castillo Ledón, who thinks that "the terminology suggested by the Belgian representative [all human beings] cover the idea which the Commission on the Status of Women is anxious to see expressed in Article 1 of the Declaration."[17]

Mr. Santa Cruz says that he:

> [F]avors the text proposed by the French representative, 'all members of the human family.' It omits the controversial statements to which he has expressed objection, it appeals to the more concrete principle of the brotherhood of men, and it fulfils the wishes of the Commission on the Status of Women, with which he fully sympathizes.[18]

The wording in Article 1 is temporarily changed back again to the initial 'members of the human family' proposed by the French delegation.

Mr. Pavlov says that there will be "difficulties in translating the expression 'all people, men and women' into Russian, as in that language women are automatically included in the notion of 'people'."[19]

These arguments raised by male delegates from both France and Russia, that women are "automatically included" in notions such as 'people,' demonstrates their blindness to how male-gendered language already is and how it is interpreted in political life to exclude women if the rights of women are not explicitly mentioned. Both male and female delegates use the word 'men' and 'man,' 'his' and 'him' throughout the debates—mostly without commenting on this gendered use of language. If, in any event, the delegates would have used 'women,' 'woman,' 'her,' and 'she' in an arguably similar "inclusive manner," it would probably have sounded absurd to most of the delegates.

The text by India and the United Kingdom is voted through in the Commission on Human Rights. Amalia de Castillo Ledón:

> [T]hanks the Commission for the amendment it has adopted to Article 1, which, although slightly different from the one proposed by the Commission on the Status of Women ["all human beings, men and women" and "in a spirit of sisterhood or brotherhood"], is in conformity with its wishes.[20]

At the outset, Article 1 of the draft Declaration prepared by the Commission on Human Rights read: "All *men* are born free, equal in dignity and rights *as human beings*, endowed with reason and conscience, and bound in duty to one another *as brothers*."[21] The second article read as follows: "All *men* are members of communities and as such have the duty to respect the rights of their *fellow men* equally with their own."[22]

The wording in Article 1 in the Declaration has now been changed to: "*All human beings* are born free and equal in dignity and rights. They are endowed by nature with reason and conscience, and should act towards one another in *a spirit of brotherhood*." Article 2 reads: "*Everyone* is entitled to all the rights and freedoms set forth in this Declaration, without distinction of any kind, such as race, color, *sex*, language, religion, political or other opinion, property or other status, or national or social origin."[23]

## Article 7 on Being Equal before the Law

The Commission is thereafter faced with a vote between two different suggestions on the formulation of Article 7 on being equal before the law—one proposed by the French delegation stating 'all men' and the other by the United Kingdom and Indian delegations simply stating 'all.' [24]

The delegations of the United Kingdom and India initially had different views on how to solve the issue of equality in the Declaration; while the United Kingdom delegation represented by Mr. Duke proposed "a footnote clarifying that every time the wording 'men' was used in the text it included women,"[25] Hansa Mehta suggested the wording in the article *itself* to be inclusive of women. She had raised the argument that in her country women would not be considered included if Article 7 read 'all men before the law.'

When the joint amendment by the delegations of the United Kingdom and India is now put to a vote in the Commission on Human Rights, Eleanor Roosevelt seems to downplay the importance of the vote on Article 7 between the French wording 'all men' and the new amendment of 'human beings.' She calls to attention that, in voting for the French version, which includes a reference to 'all men,' the Commission will be voting on form rather than on substance. She also adds that there is no "substantial difference between the French and the United Kingdom and Indian amendments."[26] The first sentence of the French amendment read as follows: "The equality of *all men* before the law is an inviolable rule." The first part of the United Kingdom and Indian amendment reads: "all are equal before the law." The French amendment is rejected seven votes to five with two abstention, and the Indian and UK amendment is adopted by twelve votes to none with three abstentions. Article 7 now reads 'all are equal before the law' (not just 'men').

## 'Let's Not Repeat Ourselves'

At a time when suffrage for women is gaining political terrain internationally in the postwar years, the Commission on Human Rights decides that non-discrimination based on sex should not be repeated in Article 21 on political rights, including the right to vote. Delegations do not explicitly oppose suffrage for women but argue that they should avoid "repetition" in the document.

The argument to avoid repetition is taken up continuously by delegations in the Commission on Human Rights in response to pressures from the Commission on the Status of Women to explicitly state in articles that human rights are women's rights. In the debate on non-discrimination regarding Article 21 on political rights (and 22 on the right to social security[27]), Amalia de Castillo Ledón declares that:

> [H]er Commission is strongly in favor of retaining the enumeration of the possible grounds for discrimination, and particularly discrimination of sex. It is unfortunately a fact that in many countries women do not enjoy political rights; the right to vote, in particular, is often withheld on the pretext of political immaturity.[28]

In the event that the Commission on Human Rights decides not to retain the enumeration of the grounds for discrimination, Amalia de Castillo Ledón wants the records of the meeting to set forth how the Commission on Human Rights interprets the word 'everyone.'[29]

If the Commission on the Status of Women had not been represented in the meetings, the Commission on Human Rights would not have had been pressured to explain their decision to omit the mention of the equal rights of women in the text.

In the final version of the Declaration, non-discrimination based on sex is only stated in Article 2 and not repeated in Article 21 on political rights, nor in Article 22 on social security—to the great misfortune of the Southern women delegates, especially of the Indian and the Latin American women delegates who will mention their frustration in the General Assembly at the final adoption.

As the Declaration has been debated at length in the Commission on Human Rights, the Commission on the Status of Women has already commended a more inclusive wording than 'all men' in Article 1, equal pay for equal work in Article 23, and the mention of non-discrimination related to suffrage in Article 21 (which failed).

It is time for the Declaration to be presented in the Third Committee for further consideration by fifty-eight delegations.

What will be up for debate next is 1) whether the preamble will state equality of women and men; 2) whether the wording 'as brothers' in Article 1 can be expressed in more inclusive language; 3) if Article 16 on equal rights 'as to marriage' can be expanded to also include divorce, monogamy, and protection against child marriage; 4) if Article 22 on social security can be changed to cover protection for mothers and children born outside of marriage; and 5) if Article 23 can mention equal pay for women and men in work.

Eleanor Roosevelt recalls in a speech at Columbia University the resistance that the Commission on Human Rights faces from several women delegates when they present their draft in the Third Committee:

> The women said . . . in this document, we are not going to say "all men" because in some of our countries we are just struggling for recognition

*Figure 7.1* J. Karam Harfouche, Lebanon. Report of the Commission on the Status of Women at the seventh session meeting of the Economic and Social Council's Human Rights Commission, 19 July 1948, *Palais des Nations*, Geneva, Switzerland.

Credit: UN Photo.

> and equality. Some of us have come up to the top but others have very little equality and recognition and freedom. If we say "all men," when we get home it will be "all men."[30]

Eleanor Roosevelt concludes:

> So, you will find in this Declaration that it starts with 'all human beings' in Article 1, and in all the other articles is says 'everyone,' 'no one.' In the body of the article it occasionally says 'his,' because to say 'his or hers' each time was a little awkward, but it is very clearly understood that this applies to all human beings.[31]

## The UDHR—Had All Proposals by the Commission on the Status of Women Been Accepted

Universal Declaration of *Human Rights*

> Preamble
> The General Assembly,

Whereas the peoples of the United Nations have in the Charter determined to reaffirm faith in fundamental human rights, in the dignity and worth of the human person and in *the equal rights of men and women* and to promote social progress and better standards of life in larger freedom, Proclaims this Universal Declaration of Human Rights as a common standard of achievement for all peoples, ***men and women***, and all nations, to the end that every individual and every organ of society, keeping this Declaration constantly in mind, shall strive by teaching and education to promote respect for these rights and freedoms and by progressive measures, national and international, to secure their universal and effective recognition and observance, both among the peoples of Member States themselves and among the peoples, ***men and women***, of territories under their jurisdiction.

Article I All *human beings* are born free and *equal* in dignity and rights. They are endowed with reason and conscience and should act towards one another in a *spirit of brotherhood* ***and sisterhood.***

Article 2 *Everyone* is entitled to all the rights and freedoms set forth in this Declaration, without distinction of any kind, such as race, color, *sex*, language, religion, political or other opinion, national or social origin, property, birth or other status. Furthermore, no distinction shall be made on the basis of the political, jurisdictional or international status of the country or territory to which a person belongs, whether it be independent, trust, non-self-governing or under any other limitation of sovereignty.

Article 3 *Everyone* has the right to life, liberty, and security of person.

Article 4 *No one* shall be held in slavery or servitude; slavery and the slave trade shall be prohibited in all their forms, ***including traffic in women and children or white slavery.***

Article 5 *No one* shall be subjected to torture or to cruel, inhuman or degrading treatment or punishment.

Article 6 *Everyone* has the right to recognition everywhere as a person before the law.

Article 7 *All are equal* before the law and are entitled *without any discrimination* to equal protection of the law. All are entitled to *equal protection against any discrimination* in violation of this Declaration and against any incitement to such discrimination.

Article 8 *Everyone* has the right to an effective remedy by the competent national tribunals for acts violating the fundamental rights granted him by the constitution or by law.

Article 9 *No one* shall be subjected to arbitrary arrest, detention or exile.

Article 10 *Everyone* is entitled in full equality to a fair and public hearing by an independent and impartial tribunal, in the determination of his ***or her*** rights and obligations and of any criminal charge against him.

Article 11 *Everyone* charged with a penal offence has the right to be presumed innocent until proved guilty according to law in a public trial at which he has had all the guarantees necessary for his ***or her*** defense. *No one* shall be held guilty of any penal offence on account of any actor omission which did not constitute a penal offence, under national or international law, at the time when it was committed. Nor shall a heavier penalty be imposed than the one that was applicable at the time the penal offence was committed.

Article 12 *No one* shall be subjected to arbitrary interference with his ***or her*** privacy, family, home or correspondence, nor to attacks upon his ***or her*** honor and reputation. *Everyone* has the right to the protection of the law against such interference or attacks.

Article 13 *Everyone* has the right to freedom of movement and residence within the borders of each State. *Everyone* has the right to leave any country, including his ***or her*** own, and to return to his country.

Article 14 *Everyone* has the right to seek and to enjoy in other countries asylum from persecution. This right may not be invoked in the case of prosecutions genuinely arising from non-political crimes or from acts contrary to the purposes and principles of the United Nations.

Article 15 *Everyone* has the right to a nationality. *No one* shall be arbitrarily deprived of his ***or her*** nationality nor denied the right to change his ***or her*** nationality.

Article 16 Men *and women* of full age, without any limitation due to race, nationality or religion, have the right to marry and to found a family. They are entitled to *equal rights as to marriage, during marriage and at its dissolution*, ***ensuring full equality in all civil rights, irrespective of marriage, nationality, race, language or religion.*** Marriage shall be entered into *only* *with the free and full consent of the intending spouses.* ***Freedom of choice, dignity of the wife, monogamy, equal right to dissolution of marriage.*** The family is the natural and fundamental group unit of society and is entitled to protection by society and the State.

Article 17 *Everyone* has the right to own property alone as well as in association with others. *No one* shall be arbitrarily deprived of his ***or her*** property.

Article 18 *Everyone* has the right to freedom of thought, conscience, and religion; this right includes freedom to change his ***or her*** religion or belief, and freedom, either alone or in community with others and in public or private, to manifest his ***or her*** religion or belief in teaching, practice, worship, and observance.

Article 19 *Everyone* has the right to freedom of opinion and expression; this right includes freedom to hold opinions without interference and to seek, receive, and impart information and ideas through any media and regardless of frontiers.

Article 20 *Everyone* has the right to freedom of peaceful assembly and association. *No one* may be compelled to belong to an association.

Article 21 *Everyone* has the right to take part in the government of his ***or her*** country, directly or through freely chosen representatives. *Everyone* has the right to *equal* access to public service in his ***or her*** country. The will of the people shall be the basis of the authority of government; this will shall be expressed in periodic and genuine elections which shall be *by universal and equal suffrage* and shall be held by secret vote or by equivalent free voting procedures.

Article 22 *Everyone*, as a member of society, has the right to social security and is entitled to realization, through national effort and international cooperation and in accordance with the organization and resources of each State, of the economic, social, and cultural rights indispensable for his ***or her*** dignity and the free development of his ***or her*** personality.

Article 23 *Everyone* has the right to work, to free choice of employment, to just and favorable conditions of work and to protection against unemployment. *Everyone, without any discrimination, has the right to equal pay for equal work.* ***Women shall work with the same advantages as men and receive equal pay for equal work.*** *Everyone* who works has the right to just and favorable remuneration ensuring for himself ***or herself*** and his ***or her*** family an existence worthy of human dignity, and supplemented, if necessary, by other means of social protection. *Everyone* has the right to form and to join trade unions for the protection of his ***or her*** interests.

Article 24 *Everyone* has the right to rest and leisure, including reasonable limitation of working hours and periodic holidays with pay.

Article 25 *Everyone* has the right to a standard of living adequate for the health and well-being of himself ***or herself*** and of his ***or her*** family, including food, clothing, housing, and medical care and necessary social services, and the right to security in the event of unemployment, sickness, disability, widowhood, old age or other lack of livelihood in circumstances beyond his *or her* control. *Motherhood and childhood are entitled to special care and assistance.* All children, *whether born in or out of wedlock*, shall enjoy the same social protection.

Article 26 *Everyone* has the right to education. Education shall be free, at least in the elementary and fundamental stages. Elementary education shall be compulsory. Technical and professional education shall be made generally available and higher education shall be equally accessible to all on the basis of merit. Education shall be directed to the full development of the human personality and to the strengthening of respect for human rights and fundamental freedoms. It shall promote understanding, tolerance and friendship among all nations, racial or religious groups, and shall further the activities of the United Nations for the maintenance of peace. Parents have a prior right to choose the kind of education that shall be given to their children.

Article 27 *Everyone* has the right freely to participate in the cultural life of the community, to enjoy the arts and to share in scientific advancement and its benefits. *Everyone* has the right to the protection of the moral and material interests resulting from any scientific, literary or artistic production of which he *or she* is the author.

Article 28 *Everyone* is entitled to a social and international order in which the rights and freedoms set forth in this Declaration can be fully realized.

Article 29 *Everyone* has duties to the community in which alone the free and full development of his *or her* personality is possible. In the exercise of his *or her* rights and freedoms, *everyone* shall be subject only to such limitations as are determined by law solely for the purpose of securing due recognition and respect for the rights and freedoms of others and of meeting the just requirements of morality, public order and the general welfare in a democratic society. These rights and freedoms may in no case be exercised contrary to the purposes and principles of the United Nations.

Article 30 Nothing in this Declaration may be interpreted as implying for any State, group or person any right to engage in any activity or to perform any act aimed at the destruction of any of the rights and freedoms set forth herein.

The French translation of the Declaration, if the suggestion by the Commission on the Status of Women defended by Chair Marie-Hélène Lefaucheux, France against Mr. Lebeau, Belgium had succeeded it would present-day be '*droits de l'homme et la femme.*' Accordingly, the French translation of the wording in the preamble would present-day be '*tous les hommes, hommes et femmes.*'

## Notes

1. Interview with Begum Hamid Ali. Lake Success, January 1949, UN Status of Women Radio Division, 1.
2. Commission on Human Rights, summary record 50th meeting, May 27, 1948, E/CN.4/SR.50, 8 (considering document E/CN.4/99).

3. Commission on Human Rights, summary record 50th meeting, May 27, 1948, E/CN.4/SR.50, 8–9.
4. Ibid., 9.
5. Ibid., 9.
6. Ibid., 9.
7. Ibid., 10.
8. Ibid., 9.
9. Ibid., 10.
10. Ibid., 10.
11. Ibid., 10.
12. Ibid., 10.
13. Ibid., 10.
14. Ibid., 10.
15. Ibid., 10.
16. Ibid., 10.
17. Ibid., 11.
18. Ibid., 11.
19. Ibid., 12.
20. Ibid., 14.
21. Commission on Human Rights, comments from governments on the draft international declaration on human rights, draft international covenant on human rights and the question of implementation, June 3, 1948, E/CN.4/82/Add.12, 24.
22. Ibid.
23. Commission on Human Rights, draft international declaration of human rights, June 18, 1948, E/CN.4/148/Add.1, 2.
24. Commission on Human Rights, summary record 52nd meeting, May 28, 1948, E/CN.4/SR.52, 6.
25. Commission on Human Rights, summary record 34th meeting, December 12, 1947, E/CN.4/SR.34, E/CN.4/57, 4.
26. Commission on Human Rights, summary record 52nd meeting, May 28, 1948, E/CN.4/SR.52, 7–8.
27. Article 22; everyone, as a member of society, has the right to social security and is entitled to realization, through national effort and international cooperation and in accordance with the organization and resources of each State, of the economic, social, and cultural rights indispensable for his dignity and the free development of his personality.
28. Commission on Human Rights, summary record 61st meeting, June 7, 1948, E/CN.4/SR.61, 16 (article 21 and 22).
29. Ibid.
30. Eleanor Roosevelt, "Making Human Rights Come Alive—March 30, 1949," Speech to Pi Lambda Theta (New York City, NY: Columbia University). Archives of Women's Political Communication, Iowa State University.
31. Ibid.

# 8 The Third Committee

## Rights in the Private Realm

> This Declaration was made with the hope that the people of the world had now reached a state of civilization and maturity to be able to honor it. . . . Those who get into power by objectionable and undemocratic means, try to remain in power by crushing dissent in flagrant disregard of human rights.[1]
>
> —Begum Shaista Ikramullah, Pakistan

Hitler had celebrated the German victory over France in 1940 by being photographed at the entrance of *Palais de Chaillot*, triumphantly overlooking the Eiffel Tower. It is now eight years later, and the defeat of Nazism and fascism is symbolically celebrated on 1 September 1948 when French Prime Minister Robert Schumann entrusts Secretary-General of the United Nations Trygve Lie from Norway with the key to *Palais de Chaillot*. The United Nations light blue flag moves in the wind in front of the Eiffel Tower with its symbolic world map and olive branches—a flag now symbolizing the freedom from the swastika that had loomed over Paris in 1940.

The final sessions of the Third Committee and the Second session of the General Assembly will be held in the most magnificent location in the heart of Paris. *Palais de Chaillot* had been built for the 1937 World's Fair, its two large, curved, colonnaded wings forming a wide arc. The central esplanade exhibits the city's greatest view of its iconic Eiffel Tower, which had been erected at the 1889 World's Fair to celebrate the one hundredth anniversary of the beginning of the French Revolution—a monument to the 'Rights of Man' and a triumph of 'brotherhood.' Will the work of the women delegates in the United Nations be acknowledged for extolling 'human rights'—as a triumph of 'sisterhood'?

Even though the United Nations has operated for two years without a permanent residence, the most spacious homes have opened one after the other for the world delegations in London, New York, Geneva, and now Paris—crowning the upcoming adoption of the Declaration with an air of historical victory. The immensity of this moment, when the flag of the United Nations is silently hoisted outside the palace and the key is handed over to the Secretary-General, should not be overlooked. Norway had been occupied by Germany during the Second World War and now sees a representative of its small nation receiving the key to the most awe-inspiring palace in Paris, *Palais de Chaillot*, on behalf of this new international organization for peace.

In the Third Committee of the General Assembly—charged with amending the drafted Declaration from the Commission on Human Rights—there are now fifty-eight delegations and more than five hundred delegates. Twelve are women delegates. Five of the women delegates in the Third Committee are also delegates to the Commission on the Status of Women: Bodil Begtrup, Denmark; Lakshmi Menon, India; Fryderyka Kalinowska, Poland; Zuloaga, Venezuela; and Minerva Bernardino, the Dominican Republic.

In September 1948, six of the women delegates in the Third Committee see the draft of the Declaration for the first time: Shaista Ikramullah, Pakistan; Ulla Lindström, Sweden; Mabel Annie Newlands, New Zealand; Margery Corbett Ashby, the United Kingdom; Marga Klompé, the Netherlands; and Aase Lionaes, Norway. All are politicians, representatives of governments. Ulla Lindström from Sweden will be the first female Acting Prime Minister in Sweden. Mabel Annie Newlands is a Labour Party activist and community leader in New Zealand. Marga Klompé will be the first female Secretary of the Netherlands. Aase Lionaes is a leader of the Labor Party Women's Organization in Norway and a long-time colleague of Secretary-General Trygve Lie. Margery Corbett Ashby is a British suffragist and President of both the International Alliance of Women (IAW) 1923–46 and of the Women's Liberal Federation in the United Kingdom. She offers her parliamentary candidature to the Liberal Party eight times, without getting elected even once into the British Parliament.

Eleanor Roosevelt is delighted to find a cooperative ally in Margery Corbett Ashby against the Soviet political insults against the Western liberal states. "England sent a new delegate to serve on the Third Committee,"[2] she says in a speech reflecting on how the Committee managed to forward the Declaration to the General Assembly.

> This delegate was Mrs. Corbett Ashby. I immediately said to her, 'Look, we have a Declaration to get through. We have spent two days listening to attacks and the answers. Do you think it is more important to get the Declaration through or to attack the U.S.S.R.?' While it is true that the Russians must be answered, Mrs. Ashby agreed that it was more important to get the Declaration of Human Rights through. By bringing the Declaration up for a vote, we would obligate the Russians to say why they had to abstain. This was more revealing for the rest of the world.[3]

In the Third Committee, there is a more crystallized difference between the British and American governments on one hand—represented by Eleanor Roosevelt and Margery Corbett Ashby—and the Southern female delegates' continuous push for women's rights in the Declaration on the other.

As representatives of the two 'Great' Western powers, Eleanor Roosevelt and Margery Corbett Ashby must endure persistent critique from the Soviet male delegates. They jointly decide on the tactic of avoiding unnecessary debates, strategically calling for votes on issues rather than holding long, passionate speeches on liberal versus socialist values, and striving toward compromise rather than ideologically based confrontation. Their goal is to have as many delegations as possible stand by the Declaration. The downside of this pragmatic stance is that women's rights—a controversial issue stirring up heated debate in the Third Committee—is not considered an apparent winning card in inspiring a majority to vote for the Declaration. Consequently, throughout the debates in the Third Committee, Margery Corbett Ashby mentions 'women' explicitly only twice—once in opposition to Saudi Arabia's delegation and their amendment of Article 16 on marriage: "of full age according to the law" as it could enable child marriages,[4] but she finds no need to repeat non-discrimination in that article. The second time Margery Corbett Ashby mentions the word 'women' is when she argues against equal advantages with men in work as she interprets 'equal advantages'[5] as meaning that women would be prevented from exceeding men.

Eleanor Roosevelt mentions 'women' once in her capacity as delegate in the Third Committee to say that women are included in 'all human beings' and once as Chair when she repeats a sentence to be voted on. In comparison, Minerva Bernardino mentions 'women' forty-nine times in the Third Committee, spanning twelve instances.

Eleanor Roosevelt will be influenced by the pressure in the Third Committee from female delegates who advocate forcefully the rights of women:

> The Third Committee has quite a number of women. Right away they saw something in our document that we brought to them which we had not given much thought to. As we presented the document, it was perhaps a little too Anglo-Saxon, a little too much like the American Declaration. It said "all men" in the beginning of a great many paragraphs.[6]

The women delegates in the Third Committee—especially delegates who are also in the Commission on the Status of Women—are unsatisfied with the preamble to the Declaration, the wording in Article 1, and equal rights in terms of marriage in Article 16.

Women delegates new to the document—from Pakistan, India, and Sweden—are attentive to the article on the right to education that is free from indoctrination, as well as making the Declaration inclusive of people without citizenship; who live under colonial rule or in trusteeships; or who are migrants, minorities, or stateless people.

According to Eleanor Roosevelt, "to pass the first three Articles in the Third Committee took four weeks and a great deal of argument, a great deal of real feeling was expressed."[7]

*Figure 8.1* Begum Shaista Ikramullah, delegate of Pakistan, Third Committee, November 1948.

Credit: UN Photo.

## Begum Shaista Ikramullah—Championing Equality of Women on Religious Grounds

Even though it is the first time she encounters the Declaration, Begum Shaista Ikramullah is no rocky in debating the rights of women, nor in drafting constitutive texts. She has served as one of only two women in the first Pakistani legislature. Her diplomatic strength lies in the fact that she has been debating women's rights with religious conservatives and found ways to stand firm in her commitment to women's equality while still being faithful to her Islamic beliefs. She has experienced both how women's rights can be compromised when women are in the minority as representatives and how religious laws and customs can be interpreted differently depending on the sex and social status of the interpreter, as she has advanced feminist Sharia laws on women's equal right to inherit property in Pakistan. Her experience bestows her manner of dealing with male Muslim delegates from Syria and Saudi Arabia in the Third Committee, specifically in debates on equal rights in marriage and on the right to education free from religious indoctrination. Her view on human rights as inclusive of women's rights differs significantly with those of the male delegates, as she affirms women's rights—both in the private and public realms.

Saudi Arabia is the only Islamic country that will abstain from voting for the final Declaration. Ten other Member States of the United Nations with large Muslim populations do not abstain but vote *for* the Declaration, including Pakistan. The other countries with large Muslim populations voting for the final Declaration in 1948 are Afghanistan, Ethiopia, Egypt, India, Iraq, Iran, Lebanon, Syria, and Turkey.

Begum Shaista Ikramullah is initially delegated to the Fifth Committee of the United Nations General Assembly, responsible for drafting the Convention Against Genocide, which works during the same time period as the Third Committee. The Fifth Committee receives far greater attention from the press, as images from concentration camps reach the far corners of the world and determination solidifies within the United Nations to create an international legal framework to combat such crimes against humanity in the future. The Nuremberg trials, held between November 1945 and October 1946, had revealed what one Jewish witness, Vasily Grossman, called "the ruthless truth of war." He testified at the Nuremberg trials regarding what he witnessed in Treblinka as a special correspondent to the *Red Star*, the Red Army newspaper. Grossman documented unsparingly how unborn babies had been burned in open wombs of dead pregnant women. "This sight could render even the strongest person insane,"[8] he writes. "Someone might ask: 'Why write about this, why remember all that?' It is the writer's duty to tell this terrible truth, and it is the civilian duty of the reader to learn it."[9]

Begum Shaista Ikramullah reminisces in her memoirs *From Purdah to Parliament*:

> In 1948 it was only three years since the Second World Was had ended. The devastation wrought by it was still fresh in people's minds—never, never again should such a thing be allowed to happen, vowed the people. It was on the lips of everybody. We must do something that will prevent the repetition of such horrors. It was with this objective in view, that two momentous resolutions, the Convention Against Genocide and

> the Universal Declaration of Human Rights was deliberated upon and passed. It was a privilege to have been associated with the drafting of these documents.[10]

The great public support for such a Convention Against Genocide placed additional pressure on the delegations representing their governments, as there was an equally strong resistance *within* the Fifth Committee by Member States who feared it would be mobilized by their own minorities. "The countries of the world that have a large number of minorities within their jurisdiction were against the passing of such a Convention, because they feared it might be used against them, unjustifiably, as a political weapon."[11]

Begum Shaista Ikramullah declares in one of the meetings:

> We cannot today sit in the comity of nations and behave in the accepted international manner and yet in our domestic matters (if it suits us) revert to barbaric practices and refuse to give an explanation of our conduct on the score of it being an internal matter.[12]

The other delegations are unmoved to change position in the debates by moral speeches as they stay with legalistic and detailed considerations to paragraphs and amendments. "I was extremely surprised when I found Sir Hartley Shawcross, an eminent jurist speaking opposite me in very complicated legal terms."[13] From this initial experience of feeling inadequate for not having studied law, she prepared her next speech meticulously regarding relevant jurisdiction. Her efforts pay off:

> When my turn came to reply, I had made myself familiar with enough legal terms to give a speech, which did not reveal my complete ignorance. I was extremely pleased when one of the members of the Fifth Committee congratulated me on my speech, and asked where I had studied Law! My entire knowledge of it was confined to Mullah's book together with Agha Shahi's explanations! This was the sum total of my legal knowledge, but I got away with it.[14]

The success of her speech notwithstanding, Begum Shaista Ikramullah is not sanctioned to continue her work in the Fifth Committee; her male colleagues feel that she received way too much appreciation for her well-prepared and magnetic speeches. She is relocated to the Third Committee, which deals with social and cultural issues. Begum Shaista Ikramullah explains:

> The delegate who was officially accredited to the Fifth Committee thought that I was getting an unfair amount of kudos, and that the Fifth Committee's work and its attendant publicity were really his due! As I did not want to be the cause of any misunderstanding and

> seeking publicity was not my objective, I went back to the Third Committee where the work on Human Rights was also very interesting and absorbing.[15]

Begum Shaista Ikramullah will stress in the Third Committee the importance of motivating political pressure upon Member States when adopting this international proclamation for human rights. If it is to live up to the name of a constitution for humanity, then national politics and prestige must give way to greater considerations.

## Revolutionary Constitutions

There are two female representatives in the first legislature of Pakistan in 1947: Begum Shaista Ikramullah and Begum Jahanara Shahnawaz. They work to get the Islamic Personal Law of Sharia approved, which recognizes the right of women to inherit property, receive equal pay for equal work, and achieve equality of social status and equal opportunities. Male colleagues object, suggesting it is a violation of Islamic law to allow women to inherit property. The law is nonetheless voted through in 1948, the same year that the Declaration is voted through in the United Nations. The approval can be credited to Pakistani women outside the legislature who protest to get it approved. The law will take effect in 1951 when the first constitution of Pakistan is adopted.

It is not only in the debate on women's rights that Begum Shaista Ikramullah raises a dissenting voice in the constituent assembly. She writes in her biography that the completion of the first constitution of Pakistan is impeded by the challenge of trying to divide the seats between East and West Pakistan; instead of trying to solve the issue, a resolution was passed stating that: "The Legislature will not enact any law which is repugnant to the Holy Koran and the Sunnah."[16] The majority pass it "with much fanfare."[17] Begum Shaista Ikramullah, however, questions the passing of the resolution; she is rather puzzled by its vague wording and inquires of the Assembly:

> [W]ho would pass a law against the tenets of Islam when the elected members of the Constituent Assembly are overwhelmingly Muslim and if by some inexplicable reason, Muslims—who form 85 percent of the population and have gone through untold suffering to establish Pakistan so that they have a state in which their culture will flourish—are to pass such a resolution, what could prevent them from doing so?[18]

Her questions and doubts are ignored by the assembly, and another resolution is introduced to safeguard the security of Pakistan. Begum Shaista Ikramullah considers "some of its clauses to be against the tenets of democracy such as the right to dissent. This to my mind was the essence of the freedom of speech."[19] The Law Minister, Mr. Brohi, attempts to persuade her to vote for the resolution on the security of Pakistan, even though Begum Shaista Ikramullah feels it dismantles freedom of speech. When the Chief Minister from East Pakistan, Mr. Amin, proclaims that with the resolution he has proposed—that no laws should contradict the Koran and Sunnah—he has done "enough for his election purposes . . . I was extremely upset and said 'In that case I will resign from the Muslim League!' "[20]

She recalls that as the proceedings began in the Hall of Assembly, "the matter was put to vote. There was a division with my solitary voice saying 'no' three times. My small voice, amplified by the microphone resounded in the large Hall of Assembly. I was alone in my dissent."[21]

Begum Shaista Ikramullah and her female colleagues intend to challenge any interpretation of Islamic law that condones discrimination against women. The passion with which they advocate can be seen in relation to Begum Shaista Ikramullah's indignation when male members of the Assembly simply refer to "no new laws against the Koran" in the discussion on citizen rights for the women and men of Pakistan—as if her dissent was not, in fact, a courageous defense of women's rights and dignity, based on another interpretation of what laws in accordance with the Koran can mean—especially for women. Contrarily, the Minister from East Pakistan feels that a general reference to Islam will cover everyone's interests.

This approach is in some ways similar to that of the drafters of the American Constitution and the French Declaration—in which men have used a general reference that, when interpreted legally, will exclude the rights of women. Begum Shaista Ikramullah's resignation from the Muslim League is thus a protest of a procedure that she felt ended the important deliberations and negotiations in the assembly.

The silencing of dissent through a blanket reference—as inclusive of all—is an expression of male authority with which many of the women in the Commission on the Status of Women are familiar, geographical differences aside.

Pakistani and Indian female representatives to the United Nations in 1947 and 1948 are taking part in the drafting of the constitutions of their countries—something that many of the Western female delegates have not. This difference is reflected in the debates in the Third Committee where the women delegates from India (Lakshmi Menon) and Pakistan (Begum Shaista Ikramullah) understand the importance of 'fundamental constitutional law,' whereas Margery Corbett Ashby feels troubled by the wording 'constitutional rights' as her country has no written constitution.[22] There is a clash at this moment in history after the Second World War in which new Member States use more progressive language in the United Nations as they have had to fight for democracy and rights, whereas in the colonial power of Britain, it had taken decades to get the right to vote interpreted as inclusive of women. The national independence movement forged alliances between women and men in Pakistan and India for achieving democracy and rights and ending colonialism.

The women's movement in Pakistan had its roots in the period before independence when the country was still under colonial rule as part of British India. The question of purdah—traditionally segregating men and women in the social and public spheres—was being forcefully contested from the time that women joined the freedom struggle.

Begum Shaista Ikramullah, coming from an influential family with liberal values and high social status, is the first female Muslim woman to graduate from the University of London. She is socially privileged to be able to question purdah and wryly dedicates the autobiography on her international career in politics to her husband "who took me out of purdah and has regretted it ever since."[23]

Begum Shaista Ikramullah and Begum Jahanara Shahnawaz are two of the prominent women engaged in the Pakistani independence movement and members of the All-India Muslim League (AIML). In 1937, Begum Jahanara Shahnawaz founded the Punjab Women Muslim League, toward which the founder of the All-India Muslim League, Muhammad Ali Jinnah, was initially negatively disposed as he did not believe in separatism but that men and women should work side by side. Women were encouraged by Muhammad Ali Jinnah to take part in the establishment of Pakistan. Pakistani women marched proudly side by side with Muhammad Ali Jinnah in the demonstrations of 1945–46. During the civil disobedience campaign in Punjab, over five hundred women were arrested in a day, but the women of Lahore continued to demonstrate for a whole month and bravely withstood violence, tear gas, and the risk of jail.

During one of the public demonstrations against British colonization, Mumtaz Shahnawaz—poet, political activist for women's emancipation, and daughter of Jahanara Shahnawaz—climbs onto the roof of the prison in Lahore and proclaims her vision of an egalitarian and democratic Pakistan. Her novel, *The Heart Divided*,[24] is a powerful narrative of a woman's devotion to politics and of questioning traditionalism, published after her death. Mumtaz Shahnawaz died at thirty-five in a plane crash on the way to a session at the United Nations in New York. Inspired by Mumtaz Shahnawaz, fourteen-year-old Fatima Sughra climbs onto the roof of the Civil Secretariat in Lahore in 1947, takes down the flag of the United Kingdom, and replaces it with the green Muslim League flag. This event was seen by many as the true moment when Pakistan was founded.

In 1947, Muhammad Ali Jinnah holds a speech for the women of Pakistan declaring that half of Pakistan is theirs as the women have expended no less effort to achieve it than the men. Muhammad Ali Jinnah's vision for a Pakistan built on reformist legislation is met with resistance from conservatives. After 1947, the progressive women's movements in Pakistan face public embarrassment from orthodox Muslim resistance groups, calling the Prime Minister's wife, Begum Ra'ana Liaqat, Ali Kahn and other women working for the All Pakistan Women Association immoral. Women's conduct that had been supported by men during the independence movement—learning self-defense and taking part in politics for democratization—is criticized by traditionalists as non-Islamic conduct after independence.[25]

In 1948, The Democratic Women Association (DWA) is founded to address working-class and under-privileged women's rights. In contrast to the All Pakistan Women Association, which was a charity organization, the Democratic Women Association is a political organization that aims to strengthen women's political and social rights. Women who have fought for independence now want a part in the political process that will frame their country.

Only six weeks after Pakistan is formally established, Begum Shaista Ikramullah is asked to represent the new country at the United Nations.

## Everyone Has a Say

The women delegates in the Third Committee who stress more inclusive language in the Declaration concerning women's rights and who insist upon the importance of the article on the rights to marriage are mainly non-Western: Minerva Bernardino, the Dominican Republic; Lakshmi Menon, India; Begum Shaista Ikramullah, Pakistan; and Mabel Annie Newlands, New Zealand, along with Bodil Begtrup, Chair of the Commission on the Status of Women. The representative of Poland, Fryderyka Kalinowska, who is also member of the Commission on the Status of Women, brings a more socialist view on women's rights and freedoms into the debate as she represents a country only recently freed from Nazi occupation.

In the draft Declaration prepared by the Commission on Human Rights to the Third Committee of the General Assembly, there is no explicit mention of equality between men and women in the preamble, as the feminist lobby at the San Francisco Conference had managed to insert into the preamble of the UN Charter. Accordingly, whereas the preamble of the UN Charter mentions equality of men and women, the draft preamble of the draft Declaration reads "the dignity and worth of the human person."[26] Moreover, the article on rights in marriage does not mention divorce, and the article on equal rights in employment does not mention equal pay for men and women[27]—all these matters are brought up in the Third Committee in relation to women's rights and by representatives from the Commission on the Status of Women to the Committee.[28]

It is late September in Paris in 1948 when the Humanitarian, Social, and Cultural Third Committee of the United Nations General Assembly holds its first meeting on the Declaration. Mr. Malik chairs the session. Eleanor Roosevelt suggests that priority be given to those delegations that have not taken part in the earlier work of the Commission on Human Rights.[29] This is a diplomatic suggestion since those who have already taken part in the drafting process at the earlier stages feel at home with the text, but for the additional Member State representatives, these wordings must still be thought through and discussed at length before all fifty-eight delegations share a sense of proprietorship of the draft, which is to be sent to a final vote in the General Assembly before the end of 1948. Bodil Begtrup suggests that the discussions in the Third Committee be limited to the Declaration and not a proposed Covenant. Her suggestion is approved, which means there will be more time dedicated to the Declaration and the Committee avoids obscuring the text by juggling legal terms between the different jurisdictional systems of the diverse delegations.

Minerva Bernardino emphasizes the importance of the democratic process in voting through a *universal* Declaration of Human Rights and seconds Eleanor Roosevelt's suggestion that the Committee first decide on having a general discussion since the Commission on Human Rights "is not composed of all Member States [and] it is quite natural that those members which were not represented on it wish to make their positions known."[30]

Eleanor Roosevelt presents the draft Declaration to the Third Committee and explains that the draft Declaration is not a treaty or international agreement and does not impose any legal obligations on the Member States.[31] This initial reassurance may have led to a greater willingness in the Third Committee to discuss human rights in a wider sense.

The Declaration, Eleanor Roosevelt continues, is rather "a statement of basic principles of inalienable human rights, setting up a common standard of achievement for all peoples and all nations."[32] In order not to downplay the importance of the Declaration for the delegations that have placed faith in the leverage of the United Nations to protect 'human rights,' she assures them that although it is not legally binding, the Declaration will nevertheless have "considerable weight."[33] Its adoption will commit Member States, in the words of the preamble, "to strive by teaching and education to promote respect for these rights and freedoms and by progressive measures, national and international, to secure the universal and effective recognition and observance." Eleanor Roosevelt reminds the Third Committee that the Declaration lists basic rights for "all men without which the full development of the individual is impossible."[34] As Chair of the Commission on Human Rights and as a representative of the United States, Eleanor Roosevelt appeals to the Committee to "strive for a majority agreement on the Declaration, and urges its members not to allow themselves to be turned aside from its goal by a search for absolute perfection."[35] Eleanor Roosevelt mentions that her delegation did not think that Article 16, "dealing with marriage, should be included in the Declaration at all."[36]

Eleanor Roosevelt has received several letters from international and American women's movements requesting that issues of women's rights and freedoms be affirmed by the drafting committee of the Commission on Human Rights. Despite the requests from the international women's lobby on this point, Eleanor Roosevelt feels that the Declaration is inclusive enough without including equal rights in marriage and to divorce. Her delegation also thinks that Article 23[37] on the right of access to public employment is "too broadly phrased,"[38] questioning the implied need for direct

*Figure 8.2* The Sub-Commission on the Status of Women. From left to right are: Hansa Mehta, India; Xu Yizhen, China; Fryderyka Kalinowska, Poland; Angela Jurdak, Lebanon; Minerva Bernardino, the Dominican Republic; Marie-Hélène Lefaucheux, France; and Bodil Begtrup, Denmark, Chair. 8 May 1946, Hunter College, New York.

Credit: UN Photo.

government intervention to uphold the economic, social, and cultural rights listed in the latter part of the Declaration.[39] That having been said, Eleanor Roosevelt concludes that the United States delegation "considered the Declaration, as a whole, a good document and is prepared to accept it in its existing form, without further amendment, if the majority so agrees."[40]

## Article 1 (Again)—Is 'All Human Beings' Inclusive Enough?

Minerva Bernardino takes the floor to make sure that the equality of women and men is the focus of the debate on Article 1 in the Third Committee.[41] "As one who has taken an active part in the international feminist movement,"[42] she thinks it:

> [A]ppropriate to remind the Committee that the question of equality between men and women has been raised at the San Francisco Conference, and that the delegations of Brazil, Mexico, the Dominican

> Republic and several other countries, submitted amendments the result of which has been the explicit recognition of that equality in the Charter of the United Nations.[43]

Minerva Bernardino says that "this has not been achieved without a certain amount of controversy; a group of delegations have held that women are included by implication in any reference to men."[44] She avers that "if the Declaration of human rights is to be of practical value for mankind, it should proclaim in the most explicit manner possible, leaving no room for doubt, that men and women are equal before the law."[45]

Minerva Bernardino advances the idea that "discrimination against any group of human beings is wrong not only because it hurt that particular group but because, in the final analysis, the fact of its existence hurts all groups in society."[46] She states that her delegation will support any version of Article 1 "which makes it clear that there is to be no 'distinction as to race, sex, language or religion'."[47]

Eleanor Roosevelt answers Minerva Bernardino by saying that the point raised "has been discussed at length by the Commission on Human Rights, and the words 'all human beings' has been used in Article 1 precisely in order that both men and women might be included."[48]

The male delegates in the Committee are more preoccupied at this point with the ideological foundation for human rights, an issue already debated in the Commission. Member States new to the drafting process want to make sure that references to their country's foundational values are mentioned. A long debate arises between secular and religious views on whether human beings are understood to be born equal. It is decided that no reference to God should be included in Article 1 when affirming the dignity of the person. The Columbian delegate Mr. Moreno adds that "reference to God could be interpreted by each country in accordance with its religious beliefs."[49] Instead of including references to different ideological grounds for human dignity and human rights, the text is stripped of any cultural or religious language that might hinder an adoption by all Member States. Article 1 is left with a simple statement on which all can agree: "All human beings are born free and equal in dignity and rights." As Mr. Matienzo of Bolivia reasons, "there was no intention of claiming that human beings were perfect. The draft Declaration was designed to set a goal for mankind. It should inspire men to transform into realities the principles it proclaimed."[50]

Minerva Bernardino is the one who turns the discussion in the Committee back to the issue of equality by replying to Eleanor Roosevelt's earlier comment, saying that she "fully appreciates the attention given to the question of the rights of women by the Commission on Human Rights and by its Chair."[51] Margery Corbett Ashby, however, adds that "no obstacles should be put in the way of the adherence of the largest possible number of countries to the Declaration."[52] With this, she seems to disavow any pressure for equality between the sexes that could hinder Member States standing behind the Declaration. Her view will be disputed by several female delegates in the Committee.

## A Declaration Nations Will Support

Reducing the text to current national legislation would be detrimental to the advancement of the rights of women in many Southern countries. The Southern women delegates want the Declaration to become a vision to which women and men aspire. Commenting on the previous debates in the Third Committee in which delegations have objected to more progressive and 'idealistic' formulations by referring to national legislation and customs, Minerva Bernardino appeals to "representatives not to bring national prejudices into the debate."[53] As the Third Committee is now composed of fifty-eight countries, Minerva Bernardino does not think it is realistic to think that they will reach a consensus or agree on all the issues, but it is preferable to focus on agreement regarding the core principles of dignity, equality, and non-discrimination. Minerva Bernardino "feels sure that the women who are participating in the work on an equal footing with men will make a great contribution towards the completion of the task."[54]

Eleanor Roosevelt seems rather tired at this point, as she has been through the debates between different countries throughout her efforts as Chair of the Commission on Human Rights, and she supports the text of Article 6 "as it stands."[55]

Margery Corbett Ashby wants "to delete the words 'without any discrimination'[56] from article six,"[57] which states that "everyone has the right to recognition everywhere as a person before the law," as she thinks this "repetition" will make people think that non-discrimination only applies to this article and not the rest. She appeals to the delegations in the Committee to take a practical attitude that will speed up the process and accept the wording in the draft by the Commission on Human Rights.

A long debate arises between male delegates of various countries on the scope on non-discrimination in the Declaration. They all agree that the second article of the Declaration is of utmost importance—although they differ in their approach in defining non-discrimination. The Soviet delegate want "class" to be included; the Indian delegate prefers "caste"; the Philippine delegate opposes class as being Marxist and caste as not being defined properly outside of India and wants to use "birth" by stating that it applies to everyone. The discussion must be ended by Chair Mr. Malik.

The women delegates from Southern countries have not responded to the male delegates' tactic of prolonging the debate by pointing to cases of discrimination in other countries and to the perfection of their own national legislation. It seems at this point that Eleanor Roosevelt wears their controversies down by firmly noting the imperfections of her own country's internal affairs and by reminding them all that they are not writing criminal law but a Declaration that is to be understood by ordinary people.

Throughout the lengthy debate amongst the male delegates on non-discrimination, 'sex' is simply not referenced. When the voting on Article 2 finally lands in the Committee, the word 'sex' in the text has not received any extra attention and is included in the final version to the General Assembly.

In this instance, silent patience seemed the best tactic to avoid controversy on the notion of non-discrimination based on sex in the text—an idea that initially had caused such dispute in the Commission on Human Rights.

## Acknowledgments

Quotes from *From Purdah to Parliament* (1998; originally published 1963) are reproduced with permission of Oxford University Press, Pakistan © Oxford University Press. Unauthorized copying is strictly prohibited.

## Notes

1. Shaista Begum Ikramullah, *From Purdah to Parliament* (Oxford: Oxford University Press, 1998), 192.
2. Roosevelt, "Making Human Rights Come Alive—March 30, 1949."
3. Ibid.
4. Third Committee, summary record 124th meeting, November 6, 1948, A/C.3/SR.124, 363.
5. Third Committee, summary record 140th meeting, November 6, 1948, A/C.3/SR.140, 526.
6. Roosevelt, "Making Human Rights Come Alive—March 30, 1949."
7. Ibid.
8. Grossman, *A Writer at War*, 301.
9. Ibid.
10. Ikramullah, *From Purdah to Parliament*, 186.
11. Ibid., 187.
12. Ibid., 191.
13. Ibid., 187.
14. Ibid., 188.
15. Ibid., 188.
16. Ibid., 198.
17. Ibid., 198.
18. Ibid., 198.
19. Ibid., 198.
20. Ibid., 199.
21. Ibid., 200.
22. Third Committee, summary record 112th meeting, October 25, 1948, A/C.3/SR.112, 237.
23. Ikramullah, *From Purdah to Parliament*.
24. Mumtaz Shah Nawaz, *The Heart Divided* (Lahore: Mumtaz Publications, 1957).
25. See further, Vrinda Narain, *Reclaiming the Nation: Muslim Women and the Law in India* (Toronto, Buffalo, London: University of Toronto Press, 2008).
26. Draft Declaration from the Commission on Human Rights to the Third Committee of the General Assembly. Preamble: Whereas the peoples of the United Nations have in the Charter determined to reaffirm faith in fundamental human

rights and in the dignity and worth of the human person and to promote social progress and better standards of life in larger freedom.
27. As had been endorsed by Evdokia Uralova.
28. Article 16; 1. Men and women of full age have the right to marry and to found a family and are entitled to equal rights as to marriage. 2. Marriage shall be entered into only with the full consent of both intending spouses. 3. The family is the natural and fundamental group unit of society and is entitled to protection.
    Article 23; 1. Everyone has the right to work, to just and favorable conditions of work and pay and to protection against unemployment. 2. Everyone has the right to equal pay for equal work. 3. Everyone is free to form and to join trade unions for the protection of his interests.
29. Third Committee, summary record 178th meeting, December 6, 1948, A/C.3/SR.178, 875.
30. Third Committee, summary record 88th meeting, September 30, 1948, A/C.3/SR.88, 29.
31. Third Committee, summary record 89th meeting, September 30, 1948, A/C.3/SR.89, 32.
32. Ibid.
33. Ibid.
34. Ibid.
35. Ibid.
36. Ibid.
37. Article 23; 1. Everyone has the right to work, to free choice of employment, to just and favorable conditions of work and to protection against unemployment.
38. Third Committee, summary record 89th meeting, September 30, 1948, A/C.3/SR.89, 32.
39. Ibid.
40. Ibid.
41. Third Committee, summary record 98th meeting, October 9, 1948, A/C.3/SR.98, 108 (considering draft declaration, article 1).
42. Third Committee, summary record 98th meeting, October 9, 1948, A/C.3/SR.98, 108.
43. Ibid.
44. Ibid.
45. Ibid.
46. Ibid.
47. Ibid.
48. Ibid., 109.
49. Ibid., 112.
50. Ibid., 113.
51. Ibid., 114.
52. Ibid., 114.
53. Third Committee, summary record 105th meeting, October 18, 1948, A/C.3/SR.105, 172.
54. Ibid., 172–73.
55. Third Committee, summary record 112th meeting, October 25, 1948, A/C.3/SR.112, 234.
56. Ibid., 235.
57. Article 6; Everyone has the right to recognition everywhere as a person before the law.

# 9 The Socialist Dissent
## A Surprising Support for Women?

> The ideas emphasized in the Declaration of Human Rights are far from being realized, but there is a goal, to which those who believe in the freedom of the human spirit can try to reach.[1]
>
> —Begum Shaista Ikramullah, Pakistan

It is now November 1948, and the Third Committee has convened over one hundred twenty-seven times since its commencement in September at *Palais de Chaillot* in Paris. Votes have been taken on both English and French versions of the text, as these were, at the time, the two working languages of the United Nations. With the inauguration of the sessions at *Palais de Chaillot*, the work of the Third Committee has received greater attention from the public, and this can be felt in the increased intensity with which the Member States scrutinize the wording of each article that comes up for debate. The Third Committee works with the aim to forward the Declaration to the General Assembly before the end of the year. There are still several sensitive issues to be resolved, and the debate has not yet reached the most visionary and controversial of the existing articles, according to the representatives to the Commission on the Status of Women—the article on marriage.

### Limit Freedom for Democracy?

The Third Committee will work not only toward increasing the scope of rights in several articles of the draft Declaration but to protect what has already been drafted from undue limitations. When Articles 18 and 19 on freedoms are debated, the Swedish and the United States delegations want to protect the freedom of thought, conscience, religion, opinion, and expression without restriction, whereas the Soviet delegation wants to have a clause stating that the freedoms of opinion and expression should be regulated within the limitations of national legislation. Begum Shaista Ikramullah of Pakistan feels that the Soviet delegation is making an uncalled-for limitation by placing the agenda of the nation state above the rights and freedoms of the individual. Fryderyka Kalinowska of Poland, on the other hand, explains the reasoning for placing limitations on the freedoms of opinion and expression, even in a democracy, by referring to the oppressive experience of occupation under fascism and Nazism when hate speech was widespread in public press.

Ulla Lindström of Sweden would like to see the text strengthened in Article 18 on the freedom of thought, conscience, and religion in order to "ensure protection of individuals against any kind of religious intolerance." She points out the "danger inherent in manifestations of political fanaticism" and the need for tolerance towards people of different religions and "those who have none."[2]

Eleanor Roosevelt fully supports the existing text on freedom of thought, conscience, and religion as she recalls it has been debated at length in the Commission on Human Rights and after "consultation with representatives of different religious organizations."[3] Eleanor Roosevelt does not respond to the Swedish proposal but declares that the United States will vote against a change to Article 18 proposed earlier by the USSR which, in her mind, limits the freedom of thought, conscience, and religion to national laws.[4] The United States is also opposed to a proposal by Saudi Arabia that Article 18 should not include the freedom to change one's religious belief.[5]

Begum Shaista Ikramullah now seems to find herself in a similar situation in the Third Committee with the Soviet amendments challenging the freedom of thought in the draft Declaration, similar to when, in the Pakistani Assembly, male colleagues had voted through laws that would undermine the freedoms for which she had fought during the independence movement. She "notes that once again the USSR delegation proposes an amendment which limits the scope of the right proclaimed by subjecting it to the special provisions of national legislation."[6] Begum Shaista Ikramullah states that the aim of the Declaration is to "define the principles which should regulate a civilized society" and that the USSR proposal to Article 19 "runs counter to that aim for it cannot be said that every national body of laws have reached the same level in the social field."[7]

Especially in relation to Articles 18 and 19, several delegations refer to national legislation as a measuring stick for governments' responsibilities to restrict freedoms. As Begum Shaista Ikramullah notes, amendments to the articles that would give precedence to existing national legislation would either lead to weaker formulations of freedoms or suppose that all nations had reached democratic and equitable societal structures. The Soviet delegation has argued that the need to uphold public order by default limits the freedom of expression and religion in Articles 18 and 19. Begum Shaista Ikramullah retorts that limitations to these freedoms are not needed in the articles themselves since the drawback clause of Article 29 already states that rights and freedoms can be restricted in order to uphold public morality.[8] Commenting on the Soviet delegation's proposals to delete the mention of 'religion' in Article 18, Begum Shaista Ikramullah wishes "to stress the necessity of not adopting any article which might shock the religious sentiments of the different peoples."[9]

Fryderyka Kalinowska proclaims that "those who were fighting against incitement to hatred and who were fighting for peace would not abandon their efforts."[10] The USSR amendment, in her view, aimed at ensuring the exercising of the rights of freedom of expression in accordance with democratic principles and in the interests of world peace. As well, she saw the amendment as aiming to prevent the propagation of fascism, aggression, and hatred.

The Soviet Union has proposed several amendments to Articles 18 and 19 that would place limitations of fascism, aggression, and hatred, but all amendments voted on by the hundred and twenty-ninth meeting have been rejected by a majority in the Third Committee, which leaves the article as it had been proposed by the Commission on Human Rights.

## Right to Education—Including Minorities?

As the debates in the Third Committee move to Article 26 on the right to education, Begum Shaista Ikramullah will support the proposals by the Commission on the Status of Women that the right to education should include the rights of minorities and non-discrimination should be repeated in the article.

Begum Shaista Ikramullah describes in her biography how the struggle for a free Pakistan had created a longing in people for freedom of thought and consciousness for which education free from indoctrination was a prerequisite. She herself had been brought up with a liberal education, and these ideas were amplified from having studied abroad and through the struggle for freedom. Outspoken about her belief that education should be free from indoctrination, she found herself in conflict both with the nationalists of her country—who wanted party politics to be taught in schools as part of history lessons—and with the religious traditionalists who opposed liberal education. She was at loggerheads with the Education Minister of Pakistan over almost every issue: from salaries of teachers to the content of education. He seemed as uninterested in her view of a liberal education then as the Soviet delegation did in the Third Committee now. "I had thought that those who had a say in forming the policy of Pakistan were people who realized the paramount importance of education,"[11] she notes in her memoirs.

Begum Shaista Ikramullah yearns to see education valued as the cornerstone of her free nation, education that could empower the populace and embody the values of a democracy they had won back after British rule. Far from everyone was enthusiastic about the progressive education she was advancing:

> The Education Minister wanted that not only religious education but party policies should also be included in the curriculum. The party

> history should be taught not in the broad spectrum of the struggle for independence but in a narrow, one-sided manner.[12]

Begum Shaista Ikramullah was saddened by this stance, viewing it as a step back:

> I felt this was a desperate situation. I had grown up in a liberal atmosphere and this attitude had gathered strength because of the Second World War which was supposed to have been fought for individual freedom and for freedom of thought and expression.[13]

During colonization, the primary objectives of education had been "to qualify or rather train one to be good civil servants in the lower grade of government service. Now the horizon had widened but the objectives remained exactly the same."[14]

When Bodil Begtrup presents an amendment to the article on the right to education, she stresses minorities' right to education and the need to repeat non-discrimination in the article.

Begum Shaista Ikramullah supports Bodil Begtrup's amendment on the right to education for minorities, as well as minorities' right to cultural expression, by adding: "It is essential to guarantee freedom to choose education, a principle flagrantly violated by the Nazis."[15] Begum Shaista Ikramullah wants the right to education to be completed with a sentence that parents have the freedom to choose their children's education (today in paragraph 3 of that article.[16]) This paragraph secures parents "only the right to choose the kind of education they wish, but not the right to withhold education from their children."[17] The Pakistani and Danish women delegates' stance is not supported by a majority in the Third Committee.

The French delegation thinks that a protection of minorities' rights is provided by Article 2 (on non-discrimination) and does not need to be repeated in Article 26. The Chilean delegation agrees—addressing the rights of minorities to start separate schools would jeopardize governments' work for unification.[18]

Begum Shaista Ikramullah parries these hesitations to minorities' rights and repetition of non-discrimination in Article 26 by conveying she would vote for an amendment merging the proposals of Denmark (Bodil Begtrup) and the Netherlands (Mr. Beaufort). Mr. Beaufort, however, does not want to merge his amendment to cover the rights of minorities, as his proposal states that parents have the right to determine their children's education.

The Soviet delegation wonders if the Committee can debate the issue of minorities later, after having considered the Soviet suggestion of repeating non-discrimination in the article, as there might otherwise be some "overlap." Bodil Begtrup withdraws her amendment on minorities' right regarding education, and it is not addressed again in the Committee.

Margery Corbett Ashby maintains that she will "vote for the basic text" if there is a consensus on it in the Committee. She objects to the USSR amendment for repeating non-discrimination in the right to education "since its substance had already been covered by Article 2."[19]

Fryderyka Kalinowska reaffirms that she will "accept the basic text with the addition of the USSR amendment." Fryderyka Kalinowska states her support for the Soviet amendment by responding to the objections: "Despite the argument that non-discrimination had been covered in Article 2, it is essential to reiterate that principle in Article 26, because access to schools in some countries is barred to certain categories of persons."[20]

The Ukrainian and Byelorussian Soviet Socialist delegations take the opportunity implied to relate how both their countries had suffered from illiteracy during the Russian Tsar empire and how now, after the Revolution in 1917, several universities had been established in the name of Socialism.

Non-discrimination is not repeated in Article 26; the Soviet delegation's amendment is voted down by a majority.

Fryderyka Kalinowska adds that she would have supported the Danish amendment, had it not been withdrawn. Poland, she says, had extended education to all minorities, after having "long suffered from discriminatory measures by occupying Powers."[21] Bodil Begtrup comments that she will resubmit the amendment later.

This will not be the case, as the question of minority rights remains too sensitive an issue in the Third Committee. Instead, Bodil Begtrup will submit a resolution to the General Assembly along with the Declaration stating that even though the Declaration does not mention the question of minorities in a specific provision, the Economic and Social Council is requested to study the problems facing minorities and suggest measures to be taken by the United Nations to address them.

The last reinforcement for a right to an education aimed at the free development of the individual is made by Latin American female delegate Zuloaga of Venezuela. Article 26[22] has "engaged the special attention" of her delegation, she affirms, "since education is the fundamental element in progress, which is the pledge of a just and lasting peace."[23] Zuloaga desires that the definition of education adopted by UNESCO be used in the Declaration, which reads:

> Education shall be directed to the full development of the human personality and to the strengthening of respect for human rights and fundamental freedoms. It shall promote understanding, tolerance, and friendship among all nations, racial or religious groups, and shall further the activities of the United Nations for the maintenance of peace.

Zuloaga "hopes that the Third Committee will decide unanimously in favor of free and compulsory education, that being the sole means of ending the illiteracy which is still widespread in the world."[24] Her proposal is unanimously adopted.

## The Preamble—Equality of Men and Women

Should the preamble of the Declaration repeat its stance on equal rights for men and women, as does the preamble of the Charter? The preamble, as drafted by the Commission on Human Rights, mentions the dignity of the person but not the equality of men and women. There will be a division in the Committee on this matter between women delegates from Poland, India, and the Dominican Republic who endorse a repetition and the American delegate, Eleanor Roosevelt, who wants the preamble to be left as is.

How is it that Eleanor Roosevelt has called all women to participate actively in governments and in the United Nations yet now does not support the explicit mention of equal rights between sexes in the Third Committee? She has already, through tedious work as Chair to the Commission on Human Rights, listened patiently to objections by delegations on endless amendments, and she is well aware of the strong opposition—held by several delegations—to the rights of women. What consequence could such an opposition have in the final vote? Eleanor Roosevelt is acting in the United Nations with the burden of a Chair's responsibility. She is under pressure from an increasing political freeze between East and West that risks hindering diplomatic communication between Member States from the two blocs. In her view, women are already included in the notion of 'human rights.'

The woman delegates who are also representatives to the Commission on the Status of Women—who have witnessed preceding debates in the Commission on Human Rights on whether to include 'equality of men and women' in the preamble—are discontented by what they consider insincerity by the delegates who use the argument of non-repetition to trump women's rights in the Declaration.

Fryderyka Kalinowska of Poland criticizes the preamble for failing to mention "the principles of non-discrimination" as well as equality between men and women, although these expressions were "included both in the UN Charter and in the body of the Declaration itself."[25] She recalls that "a number of pertinent amendments to various articles in the body of the Declaration has been rejected on the grounds that the Declaration should be clear and concise."[26] Fryderyka Kalinowska notes bitterly: "That criterion has not, apparently, been applied to the draft preamble, which contains vague and rambling generalities."[27]

Like Hansa Mehta, Fryderyka Kalinowska aspires the rights set forth in the Declaration to be upheld by legal provisions that will compel Member States to adhere to human rights. "Its lengthy introduction leads to a surprisingly weak operative clause,"[28] she observes:

> Was the work of two years by various bodies of the United Nations to result merely in urging individuals and organs of society to 'strive

> by teaching and education to promote respect for [and to] secure [the] observance' of human rights and freedoms"[29]

Eleanor Roosevelt maintains that "the fact that the Declaration will not be legally binding upon Governments makes it all the more necessary so to phrase the preamble that it will exercise upon them the greatest possible force of moral suasion."[30] She feels that Minerva Bernardino's earlier amendment to the preamble—changing "everyone" to "human person" and inserting "and in equality of rights as between men and women"—is unnecessary.[31] Eleanor Roosevelt argues that "the time has come to take for granted that such expressions as 'everyone,' 'all persons' and 'mankind' refer to both men and women."[32]

Lakshmi Menon of India affirms that her delegation "will whole-heartedly support the amendment submitted by the Dominican Republic."[33] She cannot agree "that the principle of the equality of rights between men and women will be weakened by repetition or that its general acceptance can be taken for granted."[34]

Lakshmi Menon is normally a restrained diplomat, but, when faced with weak argumentation, no matter how well intended, her criticism cuts through the room. She reminds the Chair of the Commission on Human Rights that "The United States representative has herself stated at a previous meeting that it is dangerous to use general terms since they might be misconstrued."[35] Lakshmi Menon thinks it strange that, after such lengthy deliberations in the Commission on Human Rights, it "has missed out to paraphrase 'equality of men and women' from the Charter," when the rest of the preamble is taken from that same text. She questions the arguments given for simplistic clarity in the text, stating, "It should not be forgotten, however, that even explicit laws have been rendered inoperative by judicial interpretation."[36] Lakshmi Menon recites the Fourteenth Amendment to the United States Constitution on citizenship rights as an example of this. She explains that if there is not an explicit mention of equality between men and women in the preamble, then it will be seen as "permitting discriminatory measure by nations which do not believe in the equality of the sexes."[37] Lakshmi Menon appeals "to the Committee to adopt the amendment of the Dominican Republic"[38] and insert an explicit mention of equality between men and women in the preamble.

The Southern feminist aspiration in the Committee to reformulate the preamble is held by several other Southern delegates, as well as the Soviet delegation which supports the amendment by Minerva Bernardino.

At the beginning of the next meeting, Minerva Bernardino thanks the delegations who have supported her amendment. Certain delegations had now "decided in favor of the principle," although they did "consider it was out of place in the preamble."[39] The same attitude notes Minerva Bernardino "had been shown at San Francisco during the drafting of the Charter of the United Nations."[40] She assumes that the stance is the "result of an unwillingness to grant women the same rights as those of men."[41] She asserts that she is "very persistent on this matter" because she is:

> [A]ware that the term "everyone" will not in every country necessarily mean every individual, regardless of sex. Certain countries do in fact recognize certain rights for "everyone," but experience has shown that women do not enjoy them, as, for instance, voting rights.[42]

Minerva Bernardino feels that the principle of equality in the preamble is a way to pay tribute to the heroism that women have "shown during the war."[43]

At this crucial juncture, both Lakshmi Menon and Mabel Annie Newlands reinforce the words by Minerva Bernardino. They argue that one should not take for granted that words such as 'everyone' will be read as inclusive of women in all countries—as history has shown in Western societies.

Lakshmi Menon thinks that the objection by the Chinese representative against using too much of the text from the preamble of the UN Charter is unfounded.[44] She insists that it is much more curious that 'equality of men and women' has been deleted by the Commission on Human Rights from the preamble in the draft Declaration.[45] Again, she "appeals to members of the Third Committee to affirm in the Declaration the principle of equal rights for men and women."[46]

Mabel Annie Newlands says she supports the arguments presented by the representative of the Dominican Republic and of India, whose persistence pays off in the Third Committee when the Dominican Republic's amendment is voted through by a majority.

The preamble from the Commission on Human Rights[47]:

> Whereas the peoples of the United Nations have in the Charter determined to reaffirm faith in fundamental human rights and in the dignity and worth of the human person and to promote social progress and better standards of life in larger freedom

Text of preamble adopted by the Third Committee[48]:

> Whereas the peoples of the United Nations have in the Charter determined to reaffirm faith in fundamental human rights, in the dignity and worth of the human person *and in the equal rights of men and women* and to promote social progress and better standards of life in larger freedom.

## Can We Mention Divorce?

Will the United Nations organization be looked upon as advocating divorce if equal rights for women and men in both marriage and divorce is mentioned in Article 16 of the Declaration? If this the case, then the new international organization will challenge moral values in Member States who hold the family as a sacred and integral unit of society. If the Declaration does not, however, proclaim the rights of women in the private sphere, then the United Nations will fail to address the calls from women's organizations to acknowledge the legal status of women in connection to marital status.

Debates on Article 16 in the Commission on Human Rights have been followed closely by representatives of international religious organizations. The International Union of Catholic Women's Leagues and the International Federation of Christian Trades Unions have asked the Commission "out of respect for human opinions and for Christian principles" not to mention divorce in the article. The two organizations have affirmed the need to protect the family in their pleas to omit that equality encompasses divorce.[49]

There are divergent views in the Third Committee on Article 16. For delegates to the Commission on the Status of Women, this article is of greatest importance. Eleanor Roosevelt states that her delegation thinks Article 16 should be deleted from the Declaration.

The conflicting views in the Third Committee become ever more strained as the Declaration needs approval from a majority of the governments represented in the Committee. There is a growing tension in the Third Committee between delegates who place great expectations in a Declaration of progressive formulations on equality, dignity, and rights to influence national legislation and delegates who feel that they should present to the General Assembly a document that merely reflects the sentiments and legislative traditions of Member States.

Minerva Bernardino initiates the sensitive discussion. She hopes that a member of the Commission on Human Rights will explain the previous history of Article 16[50] to the Committee and the grounds for not mentioning divorce in its first paragraph.[51]

Bodil Begtrup seconds Minerva Bernardino, inquiring how is it that the original draft that included all stages of marriage, including divorce, has been changed into merely 'marriage'?[52] Eleanor Roosevelt justifies this by claiming that "the Commission on Human Rights has interpreted the term 'marriage' in its widest sense."[53]

The representatives of the Commission on the Status of Women are not satisfied with this explanation. Article 16 is one of the "most important in the Declaration, particularly to women"[54] since marriage is a "decisive factor" in women's "social life,"[55] Bodil Begtrup affirms.

The Soviet Union has suggested an amendment to Article 16—adding after the first sentence: "Men and women shall enjoy equal rights both during marriage and when divorced."[56] In Eleanor Roosevelt's opinion, it is "unnecessary to mention within [Article 16] the principle of non-discrimination, which has been adequately covered in Article 2 of the Declaration."[57] Zuloaga of Venezuela disagrees, emphasizing that "in national law, the motives justifying divorce are not the same for men and women."[58]

She contends that the amendment by the USSR on repeating non-discrimination in the article on rights in marriage gives it "greater legal precision."[59]

The joint strategy in the Commission on the Status of Women (that Article 16 on marriage is to mention: a) the right to divorce, b) the social security of married and divorced women, c) a formulation prohibiting child marriage, and d) stating the principle of monogamy) is now voiced in the Third Committee. Bodil Begtrup calls for the Third Committee to closely study the legal and social position of women in marriage and to make sure that the Declaration emphasizes "dignity of the wife and mother, to indicate that husband and wife are on a footing of absolute equality, both legally and morally."[60] Bodil Begtrup wants Article 16 on marriage to include non-discrimination since "the dignity of the human person can only be safeguarded if every possibility of discrimination is eliminated." She wishes "equality" and "non-discrimination" to be specified "both in marriage and divorce."[61]

The French delegation defends the initial draft of the Commission on Human Rights and argues that the expression 'as to marriage' includes divorce. The French delegation reasons that the Committee should try to find a balance between progressive wording in the declaration and making it acceptable to all.

Minerva Bernardino opposes the stances of the French and American delegations. She does not believe the draft by the Commission on Human Rights affirms equality and non-discrimination. Her delegation:

> [W]ants the idea of absolute equality between men and women as to marriage, which has been accepted by all delegations, to be specifically expressed, for the nations and individuals should be able to rely not only on the spirit but also on the letter of the Declaration.[62]

Minerva Bernardino notes that:

> [T]here are countries which have not yet granted women absolute equality from the legal point of view. The ultimate goal of Article 16 should therefore be to influence governments to revise their legislation, if necessary, in order to abolish any disability affecting women in connection with marriage.[63]

Ecuador and Uruguay support the suggestion by the women delegates to the Commission on the Status of Women to mention divorce in the article.

Equal rights in marriage implies a protection against child marriage. The Saudi Arabian delegation has suggested an amendment to Article 16 that can be interpreted as permissive of child marriages. Mr. Baroody defends his proposal, stating it has been misunderstood, since national legislation would not allow this.

Mr. Baroody of Saudi Arabia claims that "the expression 'legal matrimonial age'" proposed by his delegation "takes into account the physiological aspect of the question, for in practically no country is the union of persons of non-marriageable age allowed. Moreover, exceptions to that rule can only be rectified," he argues, "by national legislation and not by a Declaration."[64] His delegation will, in any case, also accept the word 'mature' as suggested by the Syrian representative.[65]

Countering these suggestions by the Saudi Arabian and Syrian delegations, Begum Shaista Ikramullah presumes that "all civilized countries can accept Article 16," which she reads as "designed to prevent child marriage and marriages contracted without the consent of both parties, and also to ensure protection of women after divorce and the safeguarding of their property."[66] Begum Shaista Ikramullah wishes "to make it clear, however, that 'equal rights' must not mean 'identical rights'."[67] She clarifies her position by explaining that "Identical rights for women as to marriage can in some cases be a liability to them rather than an asset. That point has been ably put by the representative of Saudi Arabia," she affirms, "and the Pakistan delegation would be more than ready to support his amendment as the Mohammedan laws of marriage in all countries where they are applied give adequate safeguards to women."[68] Unfortunately, however, Begum Shaista Ikramullah cannot support the amendment, as she "fears it will enable countries with laws discriminating against women to continue to apply them."[69]

Her line of argument refutes both the critique by American delegations that 'equal rights' would mean 'identical rights' and the religious debates to safeguard personal law in accordance with religious laws. She *would* want to support an amendment to the article referring to Islamic law if that would not enable countries with laws discriminating against women to continue doing so. Begum Shaista Ikramullah manages to advocate for the rights of women on religious grounds without supporting drawback clauses to the article.

Margery Corbett Ashby wishes to keep the wording 'equal rights as to marriage.' She "opposes the Egyptian and Saudi Arabian amendments because the words 'full age' clearly implies full physical development."[70] Even though she opposes the Saudi Arabian amendment that would omit "the idea of equal rights as between men and women," she finds the USSR and Mexican amendments on repeating non-discrimination in Article 16 "equally superfluous." To repeat non-discrimination "may weaken the effect of Article 2," she argues.[71] Margery Corbett Ashby affirms that she will vote for the initial text that had been prepared by the Commission on Human Rights.

Fryderyka Kalinowska concurs with Begum Shaista Ikramullah and agrees that it must be clear in Article 16 that rights in marriage and divorce should be applied in countries without discrimination toward any group. "Since discrimination of one type leads to another," the Polish delegation thinks it "logical to condemn, together with discrimination on the grounds of sex, all other forms of discrimination that might affect freedom in marriage."[72] Fryderyka Kalinowska wishes to insert the expression "with the full consent of both intending spouses" in the article, as does Begum Shaista Ikramullah. Fryderyka Kalinowska "regrets that the United Kingdom representative opposes the USSR amendment" since she had hoped that "all women would vote for proposals affirming the equality of rights between men and women."[73]

In the vote on the amendment by the USSR and Mexico[74] (to insert 'Without any limitation due to race, nationality or religion' at the beginning of the article before the words 'men and women'), the United Kingdom and Pakistan vote against the amendment. The Dominican Republic, Denmark, and Poland vote in favor. The amendment is adopted by a majority of twenty-two votes to fifteen, with six abstentions. Several Western delegations vote against the amendment (Australia, Belgium, Canada, France, the United Kingdom, and the United States.)[75]

The following text to Article 16 is adopted by the Third Committee:

> 1). Without any limitation due to race, nationality or religion, men and women of full age have the right to marry and to found a family and are entitled to equal rights as to marriage. 2) Marriage shall be entered into only with the free and full consent of the intending spouses. Men and women shall enjoy equal rights both during marriage and at its dissolution.

## Article 23 on Equal Pay for Women

The Third Committee will find itself in a rather strange situation when it comes to Article 23 on the right to work. All paragraphs of Article 23 are adopted separately, including the USSR proposal to paragraph 2: "Women shall enjoy equal advantages in their work with men and shall receive equal pay for equal work,"[76] yet the article is rejected as a whole, with the United Kingdom and the United States voting against it. Bodil Begtrup had voted in favor of the article even though she had considered it imperfect, "precisely in an effort to avoid the ridiculous situation in which the Committee found itself, having accepted each part of the article separately and rejected the whole."[77]

The Committee cannot submit a Declaration without an article on the right to work to the General Assembly. The international labor organizations have lobbied for it as one of the most crucial articles of the Declaration that speaks to people's urgent needs in the postwar years. Through an adopted amendment to Article 23, the Soviet bloc had inserted "without distinction as to race, nationality, sex or religion" before 'the right to equal pay for equal work.'[78] The sub-committee set up by the Third Committee to draft a new version of the article, however, omits any mention of race, nationality, sex, or religion.

Lakshmi Menon of India loses her patience when the Western male delegates and the women delegates from the United Kingdom and the United

States have argued against repeating non-discrimination based on sex in the article. Although she "generally refrains from arguing on controversial issues," she feels forced on this occasion to "point out to the Committee that it is not entirely consistent."[79] Lakshmi Menon criticizes the delegations in the Committee for having adopted lengthy articles in some cases and rejecting others for the sake of brevity, for accepting certain repetitions but not others. She cannot see any rational basis behind the rejections, especially when it now came to the suggestion by the USSR and Ecuador to repeat non-discrimination due to sex in the article. "What is the real reason for refusing to repeat a clause dealing with non-discrimination?" she asks. Lakshmi Menon declares that she is not convinced by the argument that repetition will weaken the article—an argument that she fears "clouds the issue and conceals its true motives."[80] The Charter, she reminds others in the Committee, repeats "its non-discrimination clause four distinct times: in articles 1, 13, 55 and 76." New arguments need to be given for rejecting a wording that would strengthen provisions for non-discrimination against women in the Declaration. "It is no doubt difficult for Powers accustomed to regarding some races as inferior to understand and share the feelings of those who for centuries have suffered from discrimination," she declares. Lakshmi Menon insists that she cannot agree with Eleanor Roosevelt's remark "that the word 'everyone' means every human being; in many countries, it will still be understood as applying only to men; in others, as only to white men and women."[81]

Minerva Bernardino seconds Lakshmi Menon, asserting that "the right of equal pay for equal work should apply to all without any distinction. It is a principle for which Minerva Bernardino has fought for many years."[82] It is this very issue—unequal pay for women—that has sparked her feminist engagement.

The women delegates from Southern countries are backed by Southern male delegates, such as by Mr. Campos Ortiz of Mexico. He:

> [R]ecognizes the fact that some representatives regard the inclusion of a reference to the principle of non-discrimination as unnecessary and even dangerous. The majority of the Committee, however, appear to be of the opinion that the repetition of that principle is one of the most important elements of Article 23. The formal and technical arguments to the effect that such a repetition is undesirable are not relevant to a document such as the Declaration of Human Rights. Where discrimination exists, it exists particularly in regard to labor; repetition of the principle of non-discrimination will only strengthen the article on the right to work.[83]

Minerva Bernardino, perhaps strengthened by Mr. Campos Ortiz's affirmation, requests a separate vote on the word 'sex' in the article. It is rejected, however, by twenty-two votes to twenty-two, with five abstentions.[84]

At the end of the meeting, Article 23 is adopted by a majority of thirty-nine votes to one, with two abstentions. The United States votes against it while Canada and China abstain from voting on Article 23. As Chair, Mr. Malik asks delegations to explain their vote at the following meeting.

Eleanor Roosevelt explains that her delegation voted against Article 23 as a whole because it could "not accept the second sentence of paragraph two" on non-discrimination. She adds that she "fully understands the feelings of the Committee and regrets that she is unable to support the majority."[85]

Fryderyka Kalinowska explains she has voted in favor of the article since she considers "non-discrimination in the question of salaries of great importance" and she wants to pay "a tribute to the representative of India, who touched upon the crux of the problem at the preceding meeting. The best proof of the importance of the matter lay in the vote itself," she reveals.[86]

The debate on equal pay for equal work in the Third Committee overlooked the tendency for women to be relegated to lower positions and therefore earn less. Although the Second World War brought work opportunities to many women in the United States,[87] the labor movement in America would be accused of discrimination.

Bessie Hillman, Vice-President of the Amalgamated Clothing Workers, will address the persistence of this inequality when she declares at a labor meeting in 1961 that although women at that time represent a third of the work force, they are still not in power positions within the movement. Addressing the female delegates to the labor union, she comments: "Not one of you is on the executive or policy-making level of your union. Very few of you are even Presidents of locals. They let you be shop stewards, business agents, and education directors."[88]

The Third Committee finally succeeds in voting through all amended articles in the Declaration so that it could be forwarded to the General Assembly at the beginning of December in 1948. The deliberations have improved the text regarding the rights of women (the preamble and Article 16 on equal rights in marriage and at its dissolution), but in other instances, the text has had to be defended against clauses that would limit the scope of rights and freedoms (Article 26 on the right to education and Article 23 on the right to work). A majority in the Third Committee has opposed the repetition of non-discrimination in these articles, as well as the mention of specific groups that risk being discriminated against.

In response to amendments that state rights of minorities—several male delegates have declared that they would have voted for these changes in the text had it not been the case that "such rights were sufficiently covered in Article 2 of the Declaration."[89]

Article 2 was used throughout the debates as a pretense to avoid strengthening the wording on non-discrimination and equality in all the following articles. Had it not made a difference to the Declaration whether these repetitions of non-discrimination and mention of groups with special need of protection had been adopted by a majority?

Is it *evident*, as a majority of the Western male delegates and the North American and British woman delegates claim, that the Declaration and the articles address women, children, blacks, and minorities? Will anybody who reads the Declaration feel included? Is it evident that *his* and *him* applies to women? Is it evident that the right to education, to work, and to equal pay is intended without any distinction due to sex, race, or class? Would the insertion of *class* and *caste* in the Declaration be read as using a country-specific or an ideologically specific language that some argued were out of date?

Then how come the use of *his* and *him* was used; was that not specific and out of date—to see everyone as by default included in a male, white, heterosexual addressee?

The representatives to the Commission on the Status of Women in the General Assembly will voice similar objections in their closing speeches to the Assembly.

## Acknowledgments

Quotes from *From Purdah to Parliament* (1998; originally published 1963) are reproduced with permission of Oxford University Press, Pakistan © Oxford University Press. Unauthorized copying is strictly prohibited.

## Notes

1. Ikramullah, *From Purdah to Parliament*, 192.
2. Third Committee, summary record 127th meeting, November 9, 1948, A/C.3/SR.127, 390–91.
3. Ibid., 392.
4. Ibid., 392.
5. Ibid., 393.
6. Ibid., 399.
7. Ibid., 399.
8. Ibid., 399.
9. Ibid., 399.
10. Third Committee, summary record 129th meeting, November 10, 1948, A/C.3/SR.129, 419.
11. Ikramullah, *From Purdah to Parliament*, 170.
12. Ibid., 170.
13. Ibid., 171.
14. Ibid., 171.
15. Third Committee, summary record 146th meeting, November 19, 1948, A/C.3/SR.146, 584.
16. Article 26; 3. Parents have a prior right to choose the kind of education that shall be given to their children.
17. Third Committee, summary record 146th meeting, November 19, 1948, A/C.3/SR.146, 585.
18. Ibid., 588.
19. Ibid., 585.
20. Ibid., 585.
21. Ibid., 585.

22. Article 26; 1. Everyone has the right to education. Education shall be free, at least in the elementary and fundamental stages. Elementary education shall be compulsory. Technical and professional education shall be made generally available and higher education shall be equally accessible to all on the basis of merit. 2. Education shall be directed to the full development of the human personality and to the strengthening of respect for human rights and fundamental freedoms. It shall promote understanding, tolerance, and friendship among all nations, racial or religious groups, and shall further the activities of the United Nations for the maintenance of peace. 3. Parents have a prior right to choose the kind of education that shall be given to their children.
23. Third Committee, summary record 147th meeting, November 19, 1948, A/C.3/SR.147, 592 (Bodil Begtrup is Chair).
24. Third Committee, summary record 147th meeting, November 19, 1948, A/C.3/SR.147, 592.
25. Third Committee, summary record 165th meeting, November 30, 1948, A/C.3/SR.165, 761.
26. Ibid.
27. Ibid.
28. Ibid.
29. Ibid.
30. Ibid., 762.
31. Third Committee, draft international declaration of human rights, the Dominican Republic: Amendments to the draft declaration of human rights, October 4, 1948, A/C.3/217.
32. Third Committee, summary record 165th meeting, November 30, 1948, A/C.3/SR.165, 763.
33. Ibid.
34. Ibid.
35. Ibid.
36. Ibid., 764.
37. Ibid., 764.
38. Ibid., 764.
39. Third Committee, summary record 166th meeting, November 30, 1948, A/C.3/SR.166, 771.
40. Ibid.
41. Ibid.
42. Ibid.
43. Ibid.
44. Ibid., 777–78.
45. Ibid., 778.
46. Ibid., 778.
47. Commission on Human Rights, Second Session. "Draft Report of the Commission on Human Rights Submitted to the Economic and Social Council," December 2–16, 1947, E/CN.4/77, Annex A.
48. General Assembly, "Draft Report of Sub-Committee 4 of the Third Committee," December 4, A/C.3/400, Annex A Text of the Third Committee, 6.
49. Working Group on the Declaration of Human Rights, summary record 6th meeting, December 9, 1947, E/CN.4/AC.2/SR.6, 3.
50. Article 16; 1. Men and women of full age, without any limitation due to race, nationality or religion, have the right to marry and to found a family. They are entitled to equal rights as to marriage, during marriage and at its dissolution. 2. Marriage shall be entered into only with the free and full consent of the intending spouses. 3. The family is the natural and fundamental group unit of society and is entitled to protection by society and the State.

51. Third Committee, summary record 124th meeting, November 6, 1948, A/C.3/SR.124, 363.
52. Third Committee, summary record 125th meeting, November 8, 1948, A/C.3/SR.125, 367.
53. Ibid., 373.
54. Ibid., 367.
55. Ibid., 367.
56. 1. Men and women of full age have the right to marry and to found a family and are entitled to equal rights as to marriage. 2. Marriage shall be entered into only with the full consent of both intending spouses. 3. The family is the natural and fundamental group unit of society and is entitled to protection.
57. Third Committee, summary record 125th meeting, November 8, 1948, A/C.3/SR.125, 373.
58. Ibid.
59. Ibid.
60. Ibid., 367.
61. Ibid., 367.
62. Ibid., 369.
63. Ibid., 369.
64. Ibid., 369.
65. Ibid., 369.
66. Ibid., 374.
67. Ibid., 374.
68. Ibid., 374.
69. Ibid., 374.
70. Ibid., 365.
71. Ibid., 365.
72. Ibid., 371.
73. Ibid., 371.
74. Ibid., 375.
75. Ibid., 375.

    Fryderyka Kalinowska (Poland) requests that the vote on that amendment be taken by roll-call. A vote is taken by roll-call, as follows:

    In favor: Argentina, Burma, Byelorussian Soviet Socialist Republic, Chile, Czechoslovakia, Denmark, Dominican Republic, Ecuador, Ethiopia, Guatemala, Haiti, India, Mexico, Norway, Peru, Poland, Sweden, Ukrainian Soviet Socialist Republic, Union of Soviet Socialist Republics, Uruguay, Venezuela, Yugoslavia.

    Against: Australia, Belgium, Canada, China, France, Greece, Honduras, Iraq, Luxembourg, Netherlands, New Zealand, Pakistan, Syria, United Kingdom, United States of America.

    Abstentions: Afghanistan, Bolivia, Brazil, Iran, Lebanon, Saudi Arabia.

    The amendment was adopted by 22 votes to 15, with 6 abstentions.

76. Third Committee, summary record 140th meeting, November 16, 1948, A/C.3/SR.140, 536.
77. Third Committee, summary record 141th meeting, November 16, 1948, A/C.3/SR.141, 539.
78. Third Committee, summary record 140th meeting, November 16, 1948, A/C.3/SR.140, 535.
79. Third Committee, summary record 158th meeting, November 25, 1948, A/C.3/SR.158, 681.
80. Ibid.
81. Ibid.

82. Third Committee, summary record 157th meeting, November 25, 1948, A/C.3/SR.157, 682.
83. Ibid., 686.
84. Ibid.
85. Third Committee, summary record 158th meeting, November 25, 1948, A/C.3/SR.158, 692.
86. Ibid., 686.
87. "Role of Women Conference Topic," *IUD Bulletin* (July 1961), Franklin Roosevelt Library.
88. Ibid.
89. Mr. Cassin, France. Mr. Santa Cruz, Chile. Third Committee, summary record 147th meeting, November 19, 1948, A/C.3/SR.147, 587.

# 10 Is a Vote in the General Assembly a Vote for the People?

On the ninth of December in 1948, fifty-eight delegations to the General Assembly are introduced to the last draft of the Declaration in Paris at *Palais de Chaillot*. There was only one thing that could slow the adoption of the Declaration by the General Assembly before the end of the year: the Soviet delegation trying to postpone the vote to another session. The over five hundred delegates are convened in the large auditorium—a great theater hall that holds around five thousand people. All fifty-eight flags of the Member States hang ceremonially behind the podium where the President of the session is seated beside the Secretary-General.

The original fifty-one members adopting the Charter in 1945 have increased in number to fifty-eight by 1948. The Philippines and India had been represented in San Francisco and had signed the Charter, but under foreign rule. In 1948, India is one of only four Member States whose delegation is represented by a woman in the General Assembly, the freedom fighter and women's rights activist Lakshmi Menon. Pakistan, Syria, and Yemen are three other newly independent states represented in 1948.

Thirty-four delegates give speeches in the General Assembly before each article is brought to a vote. There were several flaws with the Declaration pointed out by delegates at this stage. It was not legally binding for Member States, the non-discrimination list was not repeated in the subsequent articles to Article 2, and 'him' and 'his' was used throughout the text, which could be interpreted as only addressing men.

There had been four women delegates signing the Charter in San Francisco in 1945. Now, three years later, four women delegates hold speeches in the General Assembly at the adoption of the Declaration. The wording from the preamble of the Charter, which states "equal rights of men and women" for which the Latin American feminist alliance had advocated, has been enforced in the preamble of the Universal Declaration of Human Rights.

The male delegates who give speeches to the General Assembly do not place such great importance on this historical fact in their addresses. Of the thirty male delegates who speak at the last meetings of the General Assembly before the final vote, only three mention women, and only once in their respective speeches (Cuba, Iceland, and Czechoslovakia—the last in criticizing the majority of the Third Committee). Eleanor Roosevelt, as one of the four women, does not mention women's rights.

The Commission on the Status of Women had succeeded in many of its objectives: to ensure non-discrimination based on sex, equal pay for women and men, and the right to divorce be specified in the Declaration. Three women delegates from the Commission on the Status of Women will have a final say before the vote in the General Assembly. Lakshmi Menon, Minerva Bernardino, and Bodil Begtrup all stress the importance of the equality of women in the Declaration as its most revolutionary element.

In her speech to the Assembly, Begum Lakshmi Menon declares that these rights are the expression of "a new social order, of true democracy based on social justice."[1] Neither the American Declaration of Independence nor the French Declaration included the "right to equal pay for equal work; the right of mothers and children to social protection, whether the children were born in or out of wedlock; the right to education; equality of rights for men and women."[2] She criticizes the fact that certain delegations had defended "beauty of words"[3] in their resistance to repeat non-discrimination and the equality of men and women throughout the Declaration. This was in Begum Lakshmi Menon's view merely a way to cover less pure motives as the content of the Declaration should not have been sacrificed for style. The "opposition or indifference," she says, from certain states against rights for people under colonial rule "should not be ignored."[4] She felt that "it was the duty of India, as a country which had just won its own independence, to help other countries"[5] to freedom. This vision had inspired her delegation in the debates, she says.

Minerva Bernardino articulates in her speech that she has been very persistent throughout the drafting process on speaking of the equality between men and women as a core principle of human rights. The principle, affirmed both in the preamble of the Charter and in the Declaration, "supports the legitimate aspirations of women, especially in those countries where women have not yet won their place in society."[6] Minerva Bernardino wants states to "abolish inequalities of which women are victims, based on traditional prejudices that have to give way to a more humane view that social injustice toward women affect the wellbeing and progress of the whole community."[7] Minerva Bernardino says that as world leaders do not always understand that democracy is only attainable with equality of women, she appeals to "women of the world, as well as to all women's organizations to assert their strength, to fight against the elements opposing their aspirations."[8]

Bodil Begtrup is the last representative of the Commission on the Status of Women to give a speech to the Assembly, in which she proclaims that she is convinced that "equality will set free an exceptional human force" for peace.[9] She stresses that in the Declaration before the Assembly, the word 'everyone' means every man and woman, and it would have been good to repeat that throughout the document, rather than fear criticism. She reminds the delegates to the General Assembly that the French Declaration from

1789 did not imply rights of women. "The world has evolved since then, but men tend to be conservative when in accordance with their interests."[10] She concludes by urging all the representatives present in the General Assembly:

> [T]hrough whose voice the will of the peoples is expressed not to forget that the women of the whole world are ready to collaborate with their work in peace in order to protect their homes and their children form the horrors of a new war.[11]

These last words to the General Assembly by the delegates are a reminder of the sacrifices made by women toward independence, democracy, and peace.

The draft of the Universal Declaration of Human Rights consists of a preamble and thirty-one articles. The President in the plenary meeting, Mr. Vatt of Australia, who had taken part in the San Francisco three years earlier, explains that he will "put the Declaration to the vote article by article."[12]

Article 3 of the draft Declaration stating that all rights apply to Non-Self-Governing Territories is merged with Article 2 on non-discrimination. The articles in the final text will be renumbered, consisting of thirty articles. The preamble and all subsequent articles are adopted in the initial voting round.

The text before the General Assembly in 1948 is quite different in its formulation of human rights for all regardless of citizenship. Other UN documents such as the Convention Against Genocide and the Protocol Against Drugs have special clauses providing that the rights set forth are not applicable to people living in Non-Self-Governing Territories. The Declaration, however, states explicitly in the revised Article 2 that "no distinction shall be made on the basis of the political, jurisdictional or international status of the country or territory to which a person belongs, whether it be independent, trust, non-self-governing or under any other limitation of sovereignty." This formulation is presumably made possible given that the Declaration is not legally binding on Member States—a fact that the Soviet delegation will mention in the final remark as a weakness of 'human rights' in the document.

All thirty articles are adopted, but not all are adopted unanimously: A few articles receive a nay in this round. Article 2 on non-discrimination receives one nay vote, Article 16 on rights in marriage and divorce receives six nay votes, and Article 19 on the freedom of opinion and expression receives seven nay votes, from mainly Soviet delegations.

It will take two days of meetings before the Declaration is voted on as a whole on 10 December 1948. Begum Shaista Ikramullah recalls, "Despite the delaying tactics of the Russian delegate, [the General Assembly] achieved this goal. The Universal Declaration of Human Rights was passed at midnight on 10 December 1948 by forty-eight votes to nil, with eight abstentions."[13]

When the moment arrives, delegates to forty-eight of the delegations raise their hands in the General Assembly in favor of the Universal Declaration of Human Rights in a room that holds five thousand. Are the empty seats symbolic of the exclusive diplomatic arena in which a few would represent 'everyone'?

Two countries did not vote on the Declaration as a whole: Honduras and Yemen. The eight countries who abstained were mainly Soviet states, along with Saudi Arabia and the Union of South Africa.

Mr. Smuts of South Africa had received praise for his work with the preamble to the UN Charter at the San Francisco Conference in 1945 but found himself in quite a different light in 1948. South Africa, introducing a full-fledged apartheid system in 1948, abstains from voting for the adoption of the declaration. Fryderyka Kalinowska had criticized the stance of the South African delegate Mr. Smuts in the Third Committee:

> [W]ho had contended that there was no discrimination in the courts of the Union; she wondered why, if that were so, he should object to the inclusion of a statement on the prevention of discrimination in the Declaration of human rights.[14]

Similarly, Hansa Mehta had raised in the Commission on Human Rights that delegations should not be allowed to make statements that human rights atrocities did not occur because there was no definition of human rights.

Now there would be, for the first time in history, an international document that declared that human rights included women and people under occupation or foreign rule.

Hansa Mehta and Eleanor Roosevelt would continue working together in the Commission on Human Rights to get a subsequent convention adopted. Their work was hindered by the Cold War, and the convention which would have legally bound Member States to ensure national legislation on political, civil, economic, social, and cultural rights was divided into two parts with the following two covenants: The International Covenant on Civil and Political Rights (ICCPR) and the International Covenant on Economic, Social, and Cultural Rights (ICESCR). In a like manner to how Hansa Mehta and her female colleague in the first Constituent Assembly of India had been forced to divide the Hindu Code Bill into two parts, so were human rights divided due to political ideological divisions into what would be referred to as the First and Second Generation of Rights, even though human rights were said to be indivisible, interdependent, and interrelated.

> *But still there is a Declaration of Human Rights, a Charter of human freedom, and the oppressed and their champions can at least refer to it when those who having seized the reins of power try to trample on the people. The struggle between right and wrong continues.*[15]
>
> —Begum Shaista Ikramullah, Pakistan

## Acknowledgments

Quotes from *From Purdah to Parliament* (1998; originally published 1963) are reproduced with permission of Oxford University Press, Pakistan © Oxford University Press. Unauthorized copying is strictly prohibited.

## Notes

1. General Assembly, verbatim record 182d plenary meeting, December 10, 1948, A/PV.182, 893–95.
2. Ibid.
3. Ibid.
4. Ibid.
5. Ibid.
6. Ibid., 902–03.
7. Ibid., 902–03.
8. Ibid., 902–03.
9. Ibid., 891–93.
10. Ibid., 891–93.
11. Ibid., 891–93.
12. General Assembly, verbatim record 180th plenary meeting, December 9, 1948, A/PV.180, 853.
13. Ikramullah, *From Purdah to Parliament*, 192.
14. Third Committee, summary record 112th meeting, October 25, 1948, A/C.3/SR.112, 231–32.
15. Ikramullah, *From Purdah to Parliament*, 192.

# Epilogue
## On Female Representation in the United Nations

> To know, to teach, to serve is not enough—an active participation of women in governments is what is urgently needed if the womanhood of the world is to take its rightful place. Only then can we throw in our weight for peace and outlaw war.[1]
>
> —Begum Hamid Ali, India

When the United Nations finally moves into its permanent headquarters on the East Side of Midtown Manhattan in 1952, the Secretary Building is an impressive thirty-nine-floor tower with a glass curtain wall façade.

The United Nations' second Secretary-General Dag Hammarskjöld of Sweden dislikes the disproportionately small joint prayer room for the world's delegates. The organization unites nations for peace and rights for humans from all faiths, and human rights apply to everyone regardless of religion, as its founding documents the UN Charter and the UDHR state. Dag Hammarskjöld makes a campaign for the "Friends of the UN Meditation Room" and manages to redesign it into a bigger space.

The Southern women delegates remain unsatisfied with the many compromises made to the UDHR, which have left the affirmation of women's rights in the Declaration rather implicit in several parts of the text. Consequently, the Commission on the Status of Women redirects its energies toward creating a legally binding Convention on the Political Rights of Women. Its new President, Minerva Bernardino, presents a Convention on the Political Rights of Women to the General Assembly in 1952. When the Convention is adopted by the General Assembly in 1953 (preceding the Convention on the Elimination of Discrimination Against Women, CEDAW), Dag Hammarskjöld calls Minerva Bernardino a pioneer in the field as "her work sets an example" to women who will come after.[2]

International law-making organizations have been—and continue to be—dominated by men, as noted in feminist research. The origin of human rights was, nevertheless, born as a critique of the 'Rights of Man' advocated by women delegates from Southern states fighting simultaneously for decolonization, democratization, and rights-based constitutions.

The United Nations organization reflects the politics of its Member States; accordingly, it is within its Member States populations where change for continuous emancipation and increased political representation of women has been, and continues to be, necessary.

Mary T. Norton, the first American woman Chair of a major Congressional committee, counseled American women when the Congressional elections saw female candidates run for the first time: "Don't be Sitting-Room Sarahs or Kitchen Katies,"[3] she said in an interview for a newspaper article before the elections in the United States in 1944. She herself had initially refused to run for office, claiming she was not interested in politics.[4] She later realized that any woman interested in her own family and community is inevitably interested in politics: "Women of the United States of America have never used their power. If they were to organize to their full strength their power would be tremendous."[5]

In the 1940s, women on the frontiers of religion, culture, and politics joined movements to gain suffrage. Their political advances faced a drawback in

*Figure E.1* Minerva Bernardino, the Dominican Republic; Lakshmi Pandit, India's Ambassador to Washington; and Ana Figueroa, Chile. Fifth session of the Human Rights Commission, 5 May 1949, Lake Success, New York.

Credit: UN Photo.

the 1950s. In a speech from 1953, Minerva Bernardino addresses the low representation of women in the United Nations:

> The issue is even more serious when it is observed that up to present there is not a single woman who hold a high position comparable to those of dozens of men in this world organization. Hence, we consider that the Secretary-General has not given all the proper and exact interpretation that Article 8 of the Charter requires.[6]

In a joint resolution in 1953, Venezuela and the Dominican Republic implored the Secretary-General to "appoint a greater number of women in senior and principal positions of the Secretariat of the United Nations."[7] Minerva Bernardino ended her speech by urging women to "demand to be on any national or international conference attended by men, and have the same duties and privileges."[8]

To date, only five percent of the world's countries have had at least one female leader over the past seventy years since the Universal Declaration of Human Rights was adopted.

In 1948, the Secretary-General of the United Nations was called on by the Commission on the Status of Women to appeal to the press, radio, and film industry to join in the work of ridding societies of prejudice against women.[9]

Will this call for gender parity and combating prejudice against women through the media be heeded any time soon?

I have endeavored to build upon memoirs by the women delegates, citing their works and their words from the UN meeting records. They are referenced by their full names, whereas 'Mr.' has been used to indicate male delegates. This is an inverted usage of terms to that of the United Nations records from 1945 to 1948, in which several of the male delegates were referred to by both first and last name, sometimes with professional titles. The women delegates, however, were referenced in the United Nations records as 'Mrs.' followed by their last name. Eleanor Roosevelt was referred to as "Mrs. Franklin D. Roosevelt."

Throughout this book, I have spelled out all abbreviations of United Nations bodies (with the exception of the United Nations Educational, Scientific, and Cultural Organization, commonly referred to as UNESCO, and the UN Charter). The common usage of abbreviations for conventions, declarations, commissions, and bodies within the United Nations tends to create an exclusive language—something that was not intended at the founding of the organization. All articles have been referenced in accordance with the present listing in the UDHR, www.un.org/en/universal-declaration-human-rights/

## Notes

1. Interview with Begum Hamid Ali. Lake Success, January 1949, UN Status of Women Radio Division, 1.
2. Bernardino, *Lucha, Agonía y Esperanza*, 282 (Trans. from Spanish to English), December 11, 1953, Press and Publications Office of the United Nations. At the adoption of the Convention on the Political Rights of Women, drafted mainly by the Commission on the Status of Women. The Convention on the Political Rights of Women preceded the Convention on the Elimination of All Discrimination Against Women, 1967.
3. Sam Lee, "Mary Norton Proposed for Vice President," Associated Press, *Franklin Roosevelt Library*, November 7, 1944.
4. Ibid.
5. Ibid.
6. Words of Minerva Bernardino, President of the Commission on the Legal and Social Condition of Women of the United Nations, with the theme: "Participation of women in the work of the United Nations and in the specialized agencies". New York, March 1953. Bernardino, *Lucha, Agonía y Esperanza*, 125–27.
7. Ibid.
8. Ibid.
9. "FN vill främja kvinnornas sak" [United Nations Wants to Promote Women's Issues], Geneva, August 23, 1948.

*For Zaida Catalán (6 October 1980—March 2017)*

*This book is dedicated to your memory, killed in duty for the United Nations.*

*To make human rights and peace its main mission—again.*

*Stockholm, 29 May 2017*

# Index